THE
FLOWING
GRACE
OF NOW

"*The Flowing Grace of Now* holds beautiful lessons of the heart to stir and revitalize the spiritual journey. You will find within this enriching book essays filled with wisdom, questions meant to travel deep, and prayers for humming in your soul."

Joyce Rupp
Author of *Anchors for the Soul*

"Macrina Wiederkehr's new book is a treasure to put by your bed and dip into each week. With her rich themes, questions to ponder, and wise teachers, Wiederkehr's book is for anyone who wants to make a commitment for a graced year ahead."

Christine Valters Paintner
Author of *The Soul's Slow Ripening*

"This inspiring book expertly leads us into a deepening awareness of God's wisdom flowing through various teachers offered by the present moment. Drawing on scripture and prayerful insight, Macrina Wiederkehr presents a new and sometimes startling teacher each week, guiding us to rich reflection and discovery. The final and enduring lesson comes from Wiederkehr herself, who teaches us to consciously seek and find unexpected conduits of God's grace in daily life."

Laura Reece Hogan
Author of *I Live, No Longer I*

"Week by week, day by day, breath by breath, *The Flowing Grace of Now* will open your eyes and your heart to your own life, your own journey. Sacred scripture and contemporary spiritual writings serve as twin guides yoked together by Wiederkehr's thoughtful and beautiful prose. A true gift!"

Mary DeTurris Poust
Director of Communications
Diocese of Albany

"Macrina Wiederkehr is a modern-day mystic. She shows those of us yearning for a more profound spiritual life how to make our reading of scripture truly lectio divina—sacred reading that is deeply meditative and ultimately life-changing. To make this fifty-two-week pilgrimage with such a grace-filled guide as Wiederkehr and the wisdom teachers she introduces is to allow ourselves to be transformed.

The Flowing Grace of Now might be her best book yet."

Judith Valente
Author of *Atchison Blue*

THE
FLOWING
GRACE
OF NOW

ENCOUNTERING WISDOM THROUGH
THE WEEKS OF THE YEAR

MACRINA WIEDERKEHR

SORIN BOOKS Notre Dame, IN

See Permission Acknowledgments on page 217 for notes on material used in this book.

© 2019 by Macrina Wiederkehr

www.sorinbooks.com

Paperback: ISBN-13 978-1-932057-18-8

E-book: ISBN-13 978-1-932057-19-5

Cover image © Avalon_Studio/GettyImages.com.

Cover and text design by Samantha Watson.

Printed and bound in the United States of America.

Library of Congress Cataloging-in-Publication Data
Names: Wiederkehr, Macrina, author.
Title: The flowing grace of now : encountering wisdom through the weeks of the year
      / Macrina Wiederkehr.
Description: Notre Dame, IN : Sorin Books, [2019] | Summary: "For more than
      twenty-five years, Macrina Wiederkehr has authored bestselling books on Catholic
      spirituality such as Seven Sacred Pauses and Behold Your Life and been a popular
      retreat leader. In The Flowing Grace of Now, her first book in almost a decade,
      Wiederkehr offers a weekly devotional that will reveal the spiritual teachers at
      work within your life and invites readers to sit with these teachers, learning from
      them and deepening spirituality through their wisdom"-- Provided by publisher.
Identifiers: LCCN 2019018695 (print) | LCCN 2019980557 (ebook) | ISBN
      9781932057188 (paperback) | ISBN 9781932057195 (ebook)
Subjects: LCSH: Meditations. | Spiritual life--Catholic Church.
Classification: LCC BX2182.3 .W54 2019 (print) | LCC BX2182.3 (ebook) | DDC
      242--dc23
LC record available at https://lccn.loc.gov/2019018695
LC ebook record available at https://lccn.loc.gov/2019980557

For Joyce Rupp
Kindred spirit, friend, and teacher

The Lord will give you bread in adversity
and water in affliction.
No longer will your Teacher hide himself,
but with your own eyes you shall see your Teacher,
And your ears shall hear a word behind you:
"This is the way; walk in it,"
when you would turn to the right or the left.
                                    —Isaiah 30:20–21

CONTENTS

ACKNOWLEDGMENTS

I am deeply grateful to all who have companioned me in shaping this book. There are too many of you to name. You know who you are. I bow to you and honor your insights and suggestions.

I joyfully acknowledge my monastic community as the heart of my life and inspiration. Their support has sustained me through the years.

Above all, it is a place called Bethany, one of my favorite hideaways, that I single out as my number-one source of inspiration. Bethany was a getaway house that our community once owned. Most of these reflections were originally written there in that wooded area. It was there that my teachers lived: the hawks, owls, crows, and birds of every kind; the deer and small wild animals; the pond with its resident heron; the mornings and evenings with their exuberant display of colors; and finally the starry, starry night.

Thanks to my editor, Amber Elder, for her insightful recommendations and vigilant guidance throughout this process. I am also grateful to publisher Tom Grady. It is a joy to once again work with the very fine team at Ave Maria Press.

INTRODUCTION
WAKE UP, YOUR TEACHER HAS ARRIVED

"No longer will your Teacher hide."

There is an old proverb that says, "When the student is ready the teacher will arrive." I think I have been ready for a long time, yet perhaps I have spent too much time *looking* for the perfect teacher rather than *seeing* the teachers that arrive in unexpected ways. Looking and seeing are not the same. To see requires a deeply contemplative spirit and an open heart. To see requires learning to live awake. When we realize this hallowed way of being in the world, our teacher will no longer hide. When we begin to live awake, we will see teachers everywhere. Somewhere in his vast array of writings, Thomas Merton has suggested that the most dangerous person in the world is the one who is guided by no one. Merton's wise observation has invited questions into my life: Am I open to guidance? How open? How willing am I to be taught? Do I have a heart eager for learning? Life is a wisdom school. Have I enrolled in its classes?

The ways to grow in wisdom and knowledge are endless. At this time in my life, one of my favorite ways to learn is to sit at the feet of the flowing grace of *now*. There was a time when I was apprehensive about *now*. It seemed too fleeting to learn from. It was gone before I could touch it. Countless teachers have encouraged me to make my home in the present moment. I am finally beginning to understand that to live in the moment is to live in the flowing grace of *now*. Now is not motionless and fixed; it is gracefully flowing into the next moment, the next *now*.

That's the way I learn. I lean into the moment. I lean into life. I sit at the feet of experience. I sit at the feet of life. I sit at the feet of my sins and virtues. I sit at the feet of sufferings and joys. I sit at the feet of poets, saints, and friends. I sit at the feet of beauty and brokenness—of doubt and hope. I sit at the feet of Mother Earth. I sit at the feet of the Word of God. And I listen. And I wait. And I learn.

Some of my teachers are writers and prophets whom I have never met, yet I am spiritually fed because of the insights I have gleaned from their wisdom. Thomas Merton has taught me that it is possible to be deeply immersed in the contemplative way and yet be able to speak out boldly about our need to work for peace and justice. Etty Hillesum, who died in Auschwitz in 1943, reveals by her life that it is possible to embrace love rather than bitterness. The poet William Stafford teaches me to see afresh through his ability to cause the *mundane* to blossom into something exquisite. Poet Jessica Powers mesmerizes me in her ability to find just the right words to describe my ongoing relationship with God. My own spiritual guide continues to ground me in humility as I watch him embrace the challenge of spiritual growth even in the midst of the fragility of aging.

It is difficult for me to fathom my days without the guidance of these ordinary yet extraordinary people in my life. They minister to my desire for authenticity and wisdom. They have been mentors for me, nurturing and inspiring me through the years.

Yet even in the company of these superb teachers, a kind of existential ache for God lingers in my soul. In some of my more pensive moments, I recall sitting in angst, longing for a sage or shaman to visit me from some sacred cave or aboriginal forest and feed my inquisitive mind. Such a wisdom figure, I thought, would offer answers to my eternal questions, end my unfocused living, and stir up my lethargic spirit by giving me an immeasurable supply of wisdom. That shaman or guru has never arrived in the form I was expecting, yet one morning while praying with scripture I had an overpowering realization that teachers are everywhere. This insight was as consoling as the shaman arriving on my doorstep. The scripture I was using for my prayer that day was the Mary and Martha story from the Gospel of Luke (10:38–42). I found the stirring image of

Mary sitting at the feet of Jesus therapeutic. As I visualized this uplifting image, I wondered if Jesus was also sitting at her feet—a reciprocal exchange. Were they listening to one another? Why not? That's what mature friends do.

Mary's listening annoys Martha, who is busy serving. Yet if the full truth be known, Martha was also sitting at the feet of a teacher. She was sitting at the feet of service. Later, after dinner was served, with Jesus gone and Mary retired for the evening, I envision Martha finally sitting down by herself and listening to the experience of the evening. As she reviewed the evening and her lament in the midst of her service, perhaps she began to realize that all of this was part of the wisdom offered by the school of life. We learn by contemplating our daily struggles.

Both Mary and Martha have become teachers for me. In their own way each was choosing the *better part* (see Luke 10:41). Martha inserted a bit of murmuring into her service. Her murmuring I can understand because I, too, have had to sit at the feet of my own murmuring at times. What I have learned is that when I give my authentic presence to those moments of complaining, in the form of deep listening, all becomes prayer. Life's experiences become remarkable teachers when we spend time contemplating them.

Creation is a superb teacher. Consider how parched wasteland can become a blossoming meadow after a good rain. Anticipate how you might be a rain of grace in someone's life even though there are perplexities and ambiguities in your own. You can learn from nature by listening to and reading from the pages of her landscape.

If we are attentive to the natural world around us, we may notice what an excellent teacher we have in each of the four seasons. The challenge, of course, is to live mindfully so that we do not miss the lessons hidden in the seasons. Hold each season up against your life, and look into its pages as you would look into a mirror. How can you see your face in the pages offered to you by nature's grace? Consider the little flowers growing up through deadwood. The deadwood is a source of life for them. It is their mulch. What can this teach you about the apparent deadwood of your own life? What is your mulch? What helps you grow? What can the seasons teach you?

As each new season arrives, fragments of the other seasons linger in the folds of its robes. Winter, spring, summer, and fall are mulch for each other. The seasons of our lives are like that also. We learn from the layers of life. Our joys, sorrows, regrets, hopes, miseries, and enthusiasms are mulch for each other. They nourish the future seasons of our lives. Every piece of life, every stage of growth enjoys the flowing grace of *now*—the moment when it needs to be nothing but the way it is, even as it flows into a new now.

The people with whom I live and work often serve as teachers for me. I have learned so much from watching people live. The ways they cope with their sorrows, limitations, and fears assist me as I struggle with my own weakness and flaws. I have watched people rejoice and give of themselves even in times of great drought of spirit, and I say to myself, *That's the way I want to live.* I want to learn from my pain, from my questions and unrest, from my foibles and blunders. I want to sit at the feet of those who know how to live awake. I want all of life to be a teacher.

As a Christian I claim Jesus, the Christ, as my great teacher. The scriptures offer me many insights, many teachers. When I am attentive to the Word of God speaking to me from the pages of scripture, teachers rise up and anoint me. They lead me to the hidden God within my own being. That which has been written in the prophets has proven true for me: "They shall all be taught by God" (Jn 6:45).

SUGGESTIONS FOR PRAYING WITH *THE FLOWING GRACE OF NOW*

This book is designed to be used following the fifty-two weeks of the year: one teacher a week. Each week you are to open the pages of scripture and pray with the text chosen for you. A teacher will be suggested for you. At times you may be assigned a teacher that sounds nebulous and even confusing. You may find yourself asking, "How exactly can this be my teacher?" In a sense, the entire scripture text that you are praying with is your teacher, but from the heart of that text we will single out one piece of truth for you to ponder. You are asked to prayerfully discern how that truth can be found in your life and what you can learn from it.

In your prayer, use the way of lectio divina, which is the slow, reflective reading of the scripture followed by a period of keeping vigil with the message of the text. Read the written reflection on the text, and then consider the teacher chosen for you. Is this teacher a good fit? If not, after prayerful consideration a different teacher may reveal itself to you. Ask for a teacher; then listen and wait.

You may wish to keep a journal during this year of prayer. Use it as a record of the wisdom gathered from your teachers each week. Journaling is a marvelous way to assist you in being faithful to the practice you have begun. I encourage you to be frugal in your journal entries. Sometimes less is best. Too many words get in the way, and you can't see what you're trying to say.

Pray for the grace to remain loyal to your week's theme. It is amazing how when we faithfully keep company with the Word of God, day in and day out, new insights and blessings are given us. Repetition can sometimes be a staff for our limping spirits. Thus when you are praying the daily scripture offered to you, open your heart in anticipation of a teacher with a willingness to wait for revelation.

Although you will have already read many of the scripture texts assigned in these pages, make a decision to approach the text as though hearing it for the first time. There is wisdom in standing before each scripture as though it is entirely new. Since you last read this text, most likely, many events have taken place in your life. In some small way you are not the same person.

It is always wise to take the thoughts that come to you and let them simmer in you for a while. Go deeper than what first surfaces. Let the words sink into your soul like a slow summer rain. The insight you are given on the seventh day may be substantially richer than that which you perceived on your first day. You will often notice this as you reread your journal.

> Yet just as from the heavens
> the rain and snow come down

> And do not return there
>   till they have watered the earth,
>   making it fertile and fruitful,
> Giving seed to the one who sows
>   and bread to the one who eats,
> So shall my word be
>   that goes forth from my mouth;
> It shall not return to me empty,
>   but shall do what pleases me,
>   achieving the end for which I sent it.
>   (Is 55:10–11)

When the Word of God falls into the ground of your being, you are to receive it with joy. Trust that it will do its good work in you, and it will. Let these words of encouragement from the prophet Isaiah serve as a blessing as you begin your pilgrimage through the fifty-two weeks of the year.

FIFTY-TWO
TEACHERS

These are the teachers, gleaned
from scripture,
that you will be praying with in this book.
Reference will be made to other teachers
you may encounter in the pages of your life.
The key message of this book
is that you always be open to guidance.

WEEK **ONE**

Read Psalm 16 with a heart willing to be taught.

> Protect me, O God, for in you I take
>> refuge.
> I say to the LORD, "You are my Lord;
>> I have no good apart from you."
> As for the holy ones in the land, they are
>> the noble,
>> in whom is all my delight.
> Those who choose another god multiply
>> their sorrows;
>> their drink offerings of blood I will
>> not pour out
>> or take their names upon my lips.
> The LORD is my chosen portion and my
>> cup;
>> you hold my lot.
> The boundary lines have fallen for me in
>> pleasant places;
>> I have a goodly heritage.

3

I bless the LORD who gives me counsel;
  in the night also my heart instructs
    me.
I keep the LORD always before me;
  because he is at my right hand, I shall
    not be moved.
Therefore my heart is glad, and my soul
    rejoices;
  my body also rests secure.
For you do not give me up to Sheol,
  or let your faithful one see the Pit.
You show me the path of life.
  In your presence there is fullness of
    joy;
  in your right hand are pleasures forever-
    more. (NRSV)

Psalm 16 offers us the image of a disciple who is entirely open to divine guidance. It is a prayer of candid trust—a prayer in which the psalmist claims God as protector and refuge. It is a proclamation of one who is totally surrendered to walking the path of life in God's presence. Read this psalm each day during this week. Pray it with a disciple's heart. Enter into the psalmist's words. Imagine what it would be like to allow yourself to belong to God so unreservedly that trust becomes a natural outflow of that belonging. Witness yourself taking refuge in *God* and in *good* this week. Experience the joy and comfort of trusting someone. With God as the center of your life, you will know which way to lean when the difficult times arrive. Trust even the difficult times to serve as a teacher. God will reveal the path of life for you.

As you become aware of your desire to make God your home, consider also the little gods you dally with. It happens to us all; yet those lesser gods eventually bring us unrest. Place yourself in the divine hands, and remember that your God is counselor, instructor, and teacher for you. In myriad ways you are taught by God. God's revealed presence is all around you. Don't miss it. Listen intently. Trust wholeheartedly. Rejoice always.

O God, my refuge,

The false gods of my life are not idols carved from silver and gold. They are obsessions that have been drawn from my own will. They add nothing of value to my days. They stifle the good in me. There is a path of life I must discover, a path that leads to you, my best teacher. Reveal to me the path of life that I must walk each day. Be ever with me!

Your teacher for this week is *the revealed face of God in all things.* This is a week for opening your eyes to all the wisdom that waits for you on the path of life. See teachers everywhere.

> Ask the animals, and they will teach you;
> the birds of the air, and they will tell you;
> ask the plants of the earth, and they will teach you;
> and the fish of the sea will declare to you.
> Who among all these does not know
> that the hand of the LORD has done this?
> In his hand is the life of every living thing
> and the breath of every human being.
> —Job 12:7–10 (NRSV)

WEEK **TWO**

Read Colossians 1:24–29. Claim the power of Christ's energy in you.

> Now I rejoice in my sufferings for your sake, and in my flesh I am filling up what is lacking in the afflictions of Christ on behalf of his body, which is the church, of which I am a minister in accordance with God's stewardship given to me to bring to completion for you the word of God, the mystery hidden from ages and from generations past. But now it has been manifested to his holy ones, to whom God chose to make known the riches of the glory of this mystery among the Gentiles; it is Christ in you, the hope for glory. It is he whom we proclaim, admonishing everyone and teaching everyone with all wisdom, that we may

present everyone perfect in Christ. For
this I labor and struggle, in accord with
the exercise of his power working within
me.

When I question myself as to why the marvel of
Christ living in me often remains so ambiguous,
I come face-to-face with my muddled life. I allow
myself to become too preoccupied with the vicissi-
tudes of daily life—too distracted from the heart.
The fire of Christ burns on in me, yet I forget to sit
by the fireplace. I forget to blow on the embers and
fan the flame. Thus, unfortunately, the revelation is
short-lived and loses much of its vitality because I
am negligent in keeping the fire going.

How different my days might be if I could learn
to live in the energy of Christ, who lives within
me! For this to happen, of course, I need to practice returning again and again to the center of my
life where the unfathomable mystery waits to be
embraced. Somewhere in the midst of this holy par-
adox God meets me face-to-face. Then, of course, I
die to myself, and Christ's energy in me is set free.

In Paul's short message to the Colossians, the revelation made known to you is the astounding truth that Christ lives in you. When you enthusiastically embrace the mystery of Christ living in you, Christ will no longer remain hidden but will become visible through you.

O Holy Mystery,

Though you were hidden for ages, you have now been made known, revealed in our lives. During this week, draw me into a deeper awareness of the truth that I am a vessel containing Christ-energy. Show me how to nurture your presence in me. Help me to be sensitive to the grace that surrounds me. Teach me to honor and cherish the mystery of Christ within. May it come to pass!

Your teacher for this week is *Christ's energy alive within you.* You will need to be extraordinarily mindful in order to perceive this energy. Allow yourself to be taught by the mystery of Christ living in you.

We were meant to have more
than relics of Christ.
We were meant to have,
and are meant to have,
Christ himself.

–Caryll Houselander

WEEK **THREE**

Read Matthew 15:29–31, and consider your own need for healing.

> Moving on from there Jesus walked by the Sea of Galilee, went up on the mountain, and sat down there. Great crowds came to him, having with them the lame, the blind, the deformed, the mute, and many others. They placed them at his feet, and he cured them. The crowds were amazed when they saw the mute speaking, the deformed made whole, the lame walking, and the blind able to see, and they glorified the God of Israel.

The image of people carrying loved ones in need of healing and placing them at the feet of Jesus is such a tender one. Visualize this scene and become a part of it. Let this be your prayer for the next seven days. Search your heart for every area needing healing in your life. Your need for healing may reach beyond your physical ailments to places in your spirit where you are prevented from living a wholesome life. For example, you may wish to lay before the feet of Jesus your excessive need to control or perhaps one of your feelings of resentment. Perhaps you need to place at the feet of Jesus a severe depression or a sadness that won't go away. You may bring to Jesus a terminal illness for which there seems to be no cure. The healing or cure may be a loving acceptance that enables you to live joyfully in spite of your illness. Just as the crowds on the mountaintop brought their loved ones in need of healing to the feet of Jesus, bring your physical, emotional, and spiritual limitations before him. Offer them to Jesus, the healer.

Each day this week, choose one wound that prevents you from being the joyful person God created you to be. Symbolically, lay it at the feet of Jesus; open your heart to renewal and restoration. Then ask yourself, *Do I want to be healed or cured?* I used to think healing dealt with the inner spirit while curing had to do with the physical body. Now I am not so sure. Is healing a process—something that is continuously happening to us? Does being cured mean we are entirely free to live new lives? As you place your burdens at the feet of Jesus, ponder these questions.

Jesus,

My diseases are also my dis-eases. I want to be free of these burdens. Trusting in your compassion, I lay them at your feet. I bring them to you as I would bring a precious child who needs healing. Touch my burdens with your healing presence, enabling them to become my blessing. Allow them to live in my life with a transformed face. Integrate them with my good qualities that they may become a part of the mosaic of my life. Amen.

Your teacher for this week is *your need for healing*. What can you learn from your burdens?

I am always completely astonished to discover
that I can give a nourishing talk when I feel empty,
and that I can still transmit peace
when I feel anguished.
Only God can perform that sort of miracle.

–Jean Vanier

WEEK **FOUR**

Read Psalm 19:1–7. Embrace the healing properties of both *day* and *night*.

> For the leader. A psalm of David.
> The heavens declare the glory of God;
>> the firmament proclaims the
>>> works of his hands.
> Day unto day pours forth speech;
>> night unto night whispers
>>> knowledge.
> There is no speech, no words;
>> their voice is not heard;
> A report goes forth through all the
>>> earth,
>> their messages, to the ends of the
>>> world.
> He has pitched in them a tent for the
>>> sun;
>> it comes forth like a bridegroom
>>> from his canopy,

and like a hero joyfully runs its
course.
From one end of the heavens it comes
forth;
its course runs through to the
other;
nothing escapes its heat.

This wondrous "word" that day and night continuously celebrates is, of course, the Word of God. The message that goes forth to the ends of the earth is that the Creator has covered the earth with glory. Are you perhaps called to do the same? Are you to remember that you are part of that glory?

Both day and night will serve as messengers of God for you if you can learn to pause in the midst of unfinished work. Light and darkness can become your teachers. These two messengers constantly sing the song of God's glorious presence.

Day pours forth the truth that everything is clothed in the glory of God. Yet in the midst of the *dailyness* of life, we sometimes fail to see *the day*. Look around you. What do you see that you've taken for granted? Are you aware that everything you behold has healing properties? Surely the psalm-ist who has given us this lovely poem about the wonders of creation must have realized that creation heals.

Night imparts the knowledge that darkness too is needed for growth. Some beauty can only be seen in the darkness. Some music can only be heard in darkness. Some problems can only be solved in darkness. There is a necessary darkness that assists all of life in the growing process. Night and day complement each other. Both night and day are needed in the cycle of life.

Bright Artist of the universe,

Both day and night are gifts flowing from your creative hands. The shimmering light and the darkening shadows are benevolent blessings for the soul of the earth and my soul as well. I stand in gratitude for the amazing grace of darkness and light. Reveal to me the day and night faces of my own being. Give me the desire to imitate you in covering the earth with glory. O let it be!

Your teacher for the week is *light and darkness*, day and night. Spend time with each.

> Help us to be the always-hopeful
> gardeners of the spirit
> who know that without darkness
> nothing comes to birth,
> as without light nothing flourishes.
>
> —May Sarton

WEEK **FIVE**

Read Psalm 49:5–7, 16–17 with an attentive heart.

> Why should I fear in times of trouble,
>   when the iniquity of my persecutors
>   surrounds me,
> those who trust in their wealth
>   and boast of the abundance of their
>   riches?
> Truly, no ransom avails for one's life,
>   there is no price one can give to God
>   for it. . . .
>
> Do not be afraid when some become rich,
>   when the wealth of their houses
>   increases.
> For when they die they will carry nothing
>   away;
>   their wealth will not go down after
>   them. (NRSV)

Perhaps one of the great temptations of our day is to trust in our wealth. I live in a First World country, and even though I do not consider myself wealthy, I am aware that I have opportunities and luxuries that most of the peoples of the world do not have. It grieves me that so many people want to be like us not because of noble qualities they see in our nation but rather because of material riches.

It is understandable that we would want the things that seemingly give us the *good life*, yet when we choose to dwell on that narrow aspect of wealth, we miss a larger and truer picture of life. In your estimation, what is the *good life*?

Each day this week, spend a little time contemplating the riches of your life, excluding material or financial riches. What wealth do you possess that you can't keep in the bank? What are the riches that you cannot buy? What graced gifts can you find only when you are willing to search for treasures within? What natural beauty have you failed to see around you because your mind was focused on what you are missing?

O God of so much giving,
*   My true life is all around me and within me.*
Life surrounds me and embraces me. Open the
windows of my eyes. Take away the veil that pre-
vents me from seeing the simple treasures that
are in my reach. Make me a friend of wisdom. O
may this come to be!

Your teacher for this week is *your true wealth*. Each day spend a little time with the natural riches of your life. At the end of the week make a list of the wealth you have discovered.

Above all, open the
windows wide: break
down the barriers, and
let the inside out. And
the outside in.

–Sharon Blackie

WEEK **SIX**

Read Matthew 13:1–9, keeping in mind that you are the seed being sown.

> On that day, Jesus went out of the house and sat down by the sea. Such large crowds gathered around him that he got into a boat and sat down, and the whole crowd stood along the shore. And he spoke to them at length in parables, saying: "A sower went out to sow. And as he sowed, some seed fell on the path, and birds came and ate it up. Some fell on rocky ground, where it had little soil. It sprang up at once because the soil was not deep, and when the sun rose it was scorched, and it withered for lack of roots. Some seed fell among thorns, and the thorns grew up and choked it. But some seed fell on rich soil, and produced

> fruit, a hundred or sixty or thirtyfold.
> Whoever has ears ought to hear."

As I reflect on this parable I find myself smiling at Jesus' decision to teach from a boat. He obviously didn't want to be crushed in a crowd of fans, so he got creative. Ah, a boat! Those eager to hear the Word of God stood on the shore and listened.

Try to see yourself in the crowd on that shore. Watch yourself listening to Jesus. What do you hear? This is a parable about you. You are the seed. Jesus is the sower. What is said about the seed can be said of you. Jesus has sown you into this world. You have been created and sent forth to be a blessing. Like the seed in our parable you, too, have had the unfortunate experience of ending up in the wrong places at times. You know the difficulty of trying to thrive in rocky ground. It isn't easy to put down roots for growing if you land on hard soil that's not receptive to your arrival. And getting tangled up in thorns is a smothering ordeal that is certain to snuff out any dreams you might have for a good life. All of these examples are metaphoric images that can assist you as you reflect on your efforts to grow.

However, that's not the whole story. Some of the seed fell on rich soil. Can you recognize those moments when you found yourself in the kind of soil that enabled you to grow and flourish? How did that soil differ from the hard and thorny soil?

Throughout this week you are to pray with the good soil of your life. Be grateful for the ones who have helped you blossom.

O Sower of the seed,

It is so easy for me to get obsessed about the many wrong choices I've made. It is much more difficult for me to acknowledge that I have often been obedient to my good soil. Your sowing has not been in vain, and we both know that. Open my eyes to see the many teachers who have led me to my good soil even when I was clueless to its presence. Today I am amazed at the miracle of being rooted in you. May the growth continue!

Your teacher for this week is *your good soil.* It is your holy ground. Spend time with it. Acknowledge it. Name it. Keep learning from it.

Something is waiting for us
to make ground for it . . .
so it can make its full presence known.

          –Clarissa Pinkola Estes

WEEK **SEVEN**

Read Luke 14:7–14. Read slowly, aloud, and with attention.

> Jesus told a parable to those who had been invited, noticing how they were choosing the places of honor at the table. "When you are invited by someone to a wedding banquet, do not recline at table in the place of honor. A more distinguished guest than you may have been invited by him, and the host who invited both of you may approach you and say, 'Give your place to this man,' and then you would proceed with embarrassment to take the lowest place. Rather, when you are invited, go and take the lowest place so that when the host comes to you he may say, 'My friend, move up to a higher position.' Then you will enjoy the

esteem of your companions at the table. For everyone who exalts himself will be humbled, but the one who humbles himself will be exalted." Then he said to the host who invited him, "When you hold a lunch or a dinner, do not invite your friends or your brothers or your relatives or your wealthy neighbors, in case they may invite you back and you have repayment. Rather, when you hold a banquet, invite the poor, the crippled, the lame, the blind; blessed indeed will you be because of their inability to repay you. For you will be repaid at the resurrection of the righteous."

Most of us probably don't invite friends to dinner hoping that we will be repaid. The wisdom of this parable, however, is the intimation that we are to live with pure hearts. Our actions are to flow from untainted motives. Our good deeds are not to be done to win favor, to make an impression, or even to receive thanks. If we are thanked, count it as blessing, but do not expect it. Rather, we are to live with the humility that befits a child of God. Think about your actions—why you do what you do.

Here is an exercise in humility you might want to try sometime this week—perhaps every day this week. Use your imagination and throw a banquet for the crippled, blind, and lame parts of yourself. Invite your doubts, your pride, and your superiority and arrogance. Invite your resentments, your selfishness, your narrow-mindedness, and your prejudice. In all probability, you won't find any of these invited guests trying to claim the first place. They will more likely all climb into the chair reserved for you. Here is one last suggestion. Treat each of these guests with reverence. Try to discover what this invitee is to teach you.

O lavish Caregiver,

Each day I am invited to your feast of life. Teach me to be grateful as I take my place at the table of plenty. Show me how to honor even my faults. They teach me humility. They have the potential of being transformed into something beautiful. They can become my teachers. May I learn to listen to my life.

Your teacher for the week will be *the crippled and lame parts of yourself.* Our faults and weaknesses can become our best teachers. Choose one each day this week. Try to discern why it is a part of your life.

Growth begins
when we start to accept
our own weakness.

–Jean Vanier

WEEK **EIGHT**

Prayerfully read 1 Kings 19:1–12, trying to discern the angels who feed you when you run away from your fears.

> Ahab told Jezebel all that Elijah had done—that he had murdered all the prophets by the sword. Jezebel then sent a messenger to Elijah and said, "May the gods do thus to me and more, if by this time tomorrow I have not done with your life what was done to each of them." Elijah was afraid and fled for his life, going to Beer-sheba of Judah. He left his servant there and went a day's journey into the wilderness, until he came to a solitary broom tree and sat beneath it. He prayed for death: "Enough, Lord! Take my life, for I am no better than my ancestors." He lay down and fell asleep

under the solitary broom tree, but suddenly a messenger touched him and said, "Get up and eat!" He looked and there at his head was a hearth cake and a jug of water. After he ate and drank, he lay down again, but the angel of the LORD came back a second time, touched him, and said, "Get up and eat or the journey will be too much for you!" He got up, ate, and drank; then strengthened by that food, he walked forty days and forty nights to the mountain of God, Horeb.

There he came to a cave, where he took shelter. But the word of the LORD came to him: Why are you here, Elijah? He answered: "I have been most zealous for the LORD, the God of hosts, but the Israelites have forsaken your covenant. They have destroyed your altars and murdered your prophets by the sword. I alone remain, and they seek to take my life." Then the LORD said: Go out and stand on the mountain before the LORD; the LORD will pass by. There was a strong and violent wind rending the mountains and

crushing rocks before the LORD—but the
LORD was not in the wind; after the wind,
an earthquake—but the LORD was not
in the earthquake; after the earthquake,
fire—but the LORD was not in the fire;
after the fire, a light silent sound.

Our story begins with Elijah fleeing from Jezebel. On his sojourn in the desert, he sits beneath a broom tree and prays for death. An angel awakens him, insisting that he eat so he will have strength for his journey. Nourished and strengthened by the food, he sets off on his forty-day journey to Mt. Horeb. In biblical language, mountains are almost always places of transformation. You, too, have a personal Mt. Horeb to which you must travel, a place you can go for healing and restoration. The angels who feed you along the way are not always visible. On some days it takes inexhaustible faith to believe that the nourishment you need is available.

You probably have a personal Jezebel in your life also. Your enemy may be within. Perhaps it is fear, resentment, or an unforgiving spirit. Maybe it is indifference, envy, and cynicism; perhaps it is pride, bitterness, or violent thoughts. On your journey to Mt. Horeb you want to be set free from the power of these inner enemies. There are angels along the way, intent on feeding you kindness, compassion, and courage for your desert trek.

During this week you are to become Elijah. Name your personal Jezebel. What are you running from? What kind of nourishment do you need on your way to the Mountain of Transformation? Name the angels who strengthen you along the way. Open your eyes to the ways you are fed on the way to the mountain. Envision your personal Mt. Horeb, and describe it in your journal.

O merciful One,

Lead me to the mountain. Bring me to the cave where you wait to call my name and ask, "Why are you here?" Let me hear the sound of my name spoken from your mouth. Teach me to listen, that I may find you in the silence that surrounds me. Each time I turn to you in prayer, I am on my own Mt. Horeb. Speak, Lord, and I will listen. Amen.

Let your teacher this week be *silence*. There are some things we can only learn in silence. Each day practice silence. Let it be your guide. Go to the mountain. Go to the mouth of the cave. Listen to the voice of God calling you by name.

> The practice of silence is essential
> if we wish to be wise.
>
> —Irene Nowell

WEEK **NINE**

Read Luke 13:10–17. Keep in mind the things that drain your strength.

> Jesus was teaching in a synagogue on the sabbath. And a woman was there who for eighteen years had been crippled by a spirit; she was bent over, completely incapable of standing erect. When Jesus saw her, he called to her and said, "Woman, you are set free of your infirmity." He laid his hands on her, and she at once stood up straight and glorified God. But the leader of the synagogue, indignant that Jesus had cured on the sabbath, said to the crowd in reply, "There are six days when work should be done. Come on those days to be cured, not on the sabbath day." The Lord said to him in reply, "Hypocrites! Does not

each one of you on the sabbath untie his ox or his ass from the manger and lead it out for watering? This daughter of Abraham, whom Satan has bound for eighteen years now, ought she not to have been set free on the sabbath day from this bondage?" When he said this, all his adversaries were humiliated; and the whole crowd rejoiced at all the splendid deeds done by him.

This is a gospel I understand because it is about me. Perhaps it's about you too. This woman who is badly stooped has no name, thus she can represent any one of us. Throughout this week reflect on the things that sap you of your strength. What is it that cripples you, causing you to bend over with burdens too heavy to bear?

The spirit that drains you of your strength has many names and faces. You've probably encountered all of these at one time or another. Resentments crowd out forgiveness. Fear smothers love. Indifference stifles your passion. Suspicion dampens trust. Selfishness inhibits generosity. Busyness is an enemy of presence. Jealousy dims your hospitality. Greed stifles gratitude. Anxiety enshrouds your joy. Distractions cripple your presence to God and others.

All of these heavy burdens, which you do not have to bear, will bend you to the breaking point. You can find hope as you behold this crippled woman standing up straight and giving glory to God. You, too, are invited to cast away the spirit that drains you of your strength. You can surrender many of the things that cripple you. This week you are invited to stand up straight as you walk into the healing hands of Jesus and of one another.

O healing Presence,
Into your hands I place the things that drain me of my strength. Enable me to stand up straight and walk into this new week with determination and joy. Companion me. Be my staff. You are the one I have leaned on since birth. Heal me.

Your teacher for this week will be *the bent-over person in yourself.* Bring this image to your prayer. Give a name to the things that sap your strength. Why do they drain you of your best self? Allow yourself to be taught.

On you I have depended since birth;
from my mother's womb you are my strength.

                                        –Psalm 71:6

WEEK **TEN**

Read Psalm 90, remembering the fragility of your life.

> A prayer of Moses, the man of God.
>> Lord, you have been our refuge
>>> through all generations.
>> Before the mountains were born,
>>> the earth and the world brought
>>>> forth,
>>>> from eternity to eternity you are
>>>>> God.
>> You turn humanity back into dust,
>>> saying, "Return, you children of
>>>> Adam!"
>> A thousand years in your eyes
>>> are merely a day gone by,
>> Before a watch passes in the night,
>>> you wash them away;
>> They sleep,

and in the morning they sprout
again like an herb.
In the morning it blooms only to pass
away;
in the evening it is wilted and
withered.

Truly we are consumed by your anger,
filled with terror by your wrath.
You have kept our faults before you,
our hidden sins in the light of
your face.
Our life ebbs away under your wrath;
our years end like a sigh.
Seventy is the sum of our years,
or eighty, if we are strong;
Most of them are toil and sorrow;
they pass quickly, and we are gone.
Who comprehends the strength of
your anger?
Your wrath matches the fear it
inspires.
Teach us to count our days aright,
that we may gain wisdom of heart.

Relent, O LORD! How long?
Have pity on your servants!

Fill us at daybreak with your mercy,
> that all our days we may sing for
>> joy.
Make us glad as many days as you
> humbled us,
>> for as many years as we have seen
>> trouble.
Show your deeds to your servants,
> your glory to their children.
May the favor of the Lord our God
> be ours.
>> Prosper the work of our hands!
>> Prosper the work of our hands!

Buying a birthday card for my young friend who had terminal cancer brought me to the heart of wisdom. The verses in the cards seemed utterly foolish—or so it appeared to me. I wanted to say something significant, something that mattered, yet all the words seemed uninviting, trite, and unfulfilling. Searching for words that made sense, I was brought face-to-face with my poverty. In my experience of feeling lonely and vulnerable, I begin to realize that poverty and wisdom have a connection.

My poverty calls me to reflect on past experiences. Gazing back to days of my youth, I see things more clearly. I understand life backward. It is the life I was too fearful to live that I ache for now. Perhaps rather than *counting* the days that are mine, it would be wiser *to live fully* all the days that are mine. Could this be the real invitation? In the midst of your poverty and frailty, you are to live life fully. My young friend who died of cancer did not limp through life. She lived an abundant life, and she cradled the memory of that abundant life when the difficult days arrived. Jesus was no stranger to difficult days. He, too, died young. Is it how long we live or how wisely we live that matters in the end? Ponder these things and gain wisdom of heart.

Author of our lives,

You fashioned us from the stardust of the earth. Thank you for the fragility and impermanence of all that is created. I want to be faithful to the beauty that hides even in that which is fleeting and transient. Today I recall all I have learned from my fragility. When I can learn from my own weakness, then I will be able to understand how the broken vessel of another person's life can also be my teacher. Open my eyes to the beauty of all that is ephemeral. O let it be!

Your teacher for the week is *your daily life*. Choose one thing each day and approach it with reverence. Offer it your presence. Watch yourself live. Let life teach you.

It's Friday afternoon and the sun is out,
but I have so much on my desk and if I stay till 6 or 7
I can start next week ahead of things
but the sun is so bright,
my heart begging me to burst into the day
and now a small yellowish bird
is flirting outside my window. . . .
I wonder why it is so hard to put things down and live.
                                         —Mark Nepo

WEEK **ELEVEN**

Take off your shoes, and read Exodus 3:1–7.

> Meanwhile Moses was tending the flock of his father-in-law Jethro, the priest of Midian. Leading the flock beyond the wilderness, he came to the mountain of God, Horeb. There the angel of the LORD appeared to him as fire flaming out of a bush. When he looked, although the bush was on fire, it was not being consumed. So Moses decided, "I must turn aside to look at this remarkable sight. Why does the bush not burn up?" When the LORD saw that he had turned aside to look, God called out to him from the bush: Moses! Moses! He answered, "Here I am." God said: Do not come near! Remove your sandals from your feet, for the place where you

stand is holy ground. I am the God of
your father, he continued, the God of
Abraham, the God of Isaac, and the God
of Jacob. Moses hid his face, for he was
afraid to look at God.

But the LORD said: I have witnessed
the affliction of my people in Egypt and
have heard their cry against their task-
masters, so I know well what they are
suffering.

Moses: rescued from the waters, growing up in lux-
ury, returning to his ancestors. He finally becomes a
runaway in the wilderness. The burning bush called
him to attention and to further exploration. Desir-
ing to understand the flaming wonder before him,
he draws closer. He investigates and discovers that
at the heart of this mystery is *The One Who Cannot
Be Named*. It's a revelation, a theophany, and a call.

You, too, are a burning bush. In whatever season
of life you find yourself, you are invited to explore
your deep self. What marvels within are gazing at
you, waiting for your curiosity and investigation?
Move closer to contemplate your own mysterious
flame. What do you need to turn away from in order

to see more clearly who you really are? What do you need to turn toward so that you may be drawn into a richer experience of the divine mystery? What do you need to turn away from so that you can hear the voice of God?

O sacred Fire,

You have created in me a resemblance of the divine image. It is not easy for me to claim that honor. I hesitate to own the flame of life you have bequeathed to me. Open my eyes to the holy ground of my own being and to the burning bushes of those around me. Like Moses, I want to investigate the intriguing mystery. I want to accept your invitation to draw closer and to take off my shoes. It is time for my own theophany. Let there be fire.

Your teacher for this week is *the burning bush*. Look for it everywhere: in yourself, in others, in your experiences, and in nature. Wherever you find it, do what Moses did. Take off your shoes. Open yourself to revelation. Allow yourself to be taught.

When we are capable of stopping
we begin to see.

–Thich Nhat Hanh

WEEK **TWELVE**

Slowly read Isaiah 49:1–6.

> Hear me, coastlands,
>> listen, distant peoples.
> Before birth the LORD called me,
>> from my mother's womb he gave me
>>> my name.
> He made my mouth like a sharp-edged
>>> sword,
>> concealed me, shielded by his hand.
> He made me a sharpened arrow,
>> in his quiver he hid me.
> He said to me, You are my servant,
>> in you, Israel, I show my glory.
> Though I thought I had toiled in vain,
>> for nothing and for naught spent my
>>> strength,
> Yet my right is with the LORD,
>> my recompense is with my God.
> For now the LORD has spoken

> who formed me as his servant from
> > the womb,
> That Jacob may be brought back to him
> > and Israel gathered to him;
> I am honored in the sight of the LORD,
> > and my God is now my strength!
> It is too little, he says, for you to be my
> > servant,
> > to raise up the tribes of Jacob,
> > and restore the survivors of Israel;
> I will make you a light to the nations,
> > that my salvation may reach to the ends
> > > of the earth.

Isaiah speaks confidently about being called from birth and clothed with a name. The idea of being intimately known while still in the womb is mesmerizing. Take a few moments as part of your prayer to ponder this concept as a reality. Have you ever had a sense of being intimately known by God while still in the womb? Listen intently to that question. And what about the name God gave you?

It is an *inner name* that is being referred to in this text. The servant of God speaks of coming forth from the womb bearing a divine imprint. Doing the work of God is not always easy, yet the voice rising out of this text proclaims the truth of an ancient inner strength that abides in human flesh. God is revealed as a companioning presence from birth and as the One who gives us our name.

Each of us has a name deeper than the name given us by our parents. It is an *inner name*, etched in the soul. Unlike our DNA it cannot be measured or recorded; it can only be revealed and discovered—and eventually proclaimed and lived.

Throughout this week, ponder your unknown name. Hold dear the name given you at birth even as you listen for your *new name*. Choose a name that speaks of your call to be authentic. Choose a name that echoes your invitation to be both servant and prophet. Or let the name choose you. Pray to be enlightened in regard to your own prophetic-servant vocation. What were you born to say? Why have you been sent to planet Earth? Listen for the Divine Voice! What is your name? Cherish it.

My inner name came to me many moons ago while leading a retreat in southern California. I didn't hear an actual voice calling out my name. It

was more like a little bell ringing in my heart's ear.
It rang out crystal clear: Joyous Clay, Joyous Clay!
And now I live my life trying to be that joyous clay.

O birth-giving God,
    *Let me hear the name you gave me in my
mother's womb. Help me discover the words I
was born to proclaim. Teach me to honor my
daily birth into your love. Amen.*

Your teacher for this week is *your inner name*. Listen
carefully each day for that hidden name. Until you
find it, let your birth name teach you.

> We need to exercise great care and respect
> when we come to name something.
> We always need to find a name
> that is worthy and spacious.
> When we name things in a small way,
> we cripple them.
> > —John O'Donohue

WEEK **THIRTEEN**

Read Colossians 1:1–8 as though the text was written just for you.

> Paul, an apostle of Christ Jesus by the will of God, and Timothy our brother, to the holy ones and faithful brothers in Christ in Colossae: grace to you and peace from God our Father.
>
> We always give thanks to God, the Father of our Lord Jesus Christ, when we pray for you, for we have heard of your faith in Christ Jesus and the love that you have for all the holy ones because of the hope reserved for you in heaven. Of this you have already heard through the word of truth, the Gospel, that has come to you. Just as in the whole world it is bearing fruit and growing, so also among you, from the day you heard it and came to

> know the grace of God in truth, as you
> learned it from Epaphras our beloved fel-
> low slave, who is a trustworthy minister of
> Christ on your behalf and who also told
> us of your love in the Spirit.

Those of us who are struggling to be true to the faith
we've absorbed from our teachers benefit greatly
from a steady flow of encouragement. We all need to
know that someone believes in us and cherishes our
spiritual growth. We need to hear that we are mak-
ing a little progress. In this short text from Paul's
letter to the Colossians, it is obvious he is experi-
encing delight and gratitude because of the people's
progress in the way of Christ. He offers support
to these new Christians using words of gratitude
for their faithfulness, assuring them they are being
remembered to God. Paul reminds them that just as
the Gospel is spreading across the world and bearing
fruit, the same is happening in their individual lives.

Throughout this week, spend some time each
day reflecting on your faith life. Read Colossians
1:1–8 as though it were being read to you by one of
your favorite saints or perhaps one of your teachers

or a spiritual guide. Can you own the truth that good things are happening in your life? What are some of the ways you've made progress in the past month? How do you need to be encouraged? In what areas do you need a little challenge? Who are some of the people responsible for lifting you up when your faith is wavering? Let this be a week of deepening your faith and being grateful for the Christ of faith who abides in you.

Christ, my life, my guide, my teacher,

Gratitude for your faithful presence fills my soul. Just as I have faith in you, I am confident that you have faith in me. The Word of God gives me immense hope and joy. It is because of this gift that I expect to bear fruit in my life. Bless those who have supported me on my spiritual journey. Amen.

Your teachers for this week are *those who have encouraged you*. Let their faces appear before you. Envision them. Name them. Inscribe their names and the

ways they have encouraged you in your journal.
Speak to them.

> Therefore, encourage one another
> and build one another up,
> as indeed you do.
>
> —1 Thessalonians 5:11

WEEK **FOURTEEN**

Read Matthew 15:21–28 with the same buoyant spirit as that of the Canaanite woman.

> Then Jesus went from that place and withdrew to the region of Tyre and Sidon. And behold, a Canaanite woman of that district came and called out, "Have pity on me, Lord, Son of David! My daughter is tormented by a demon." But he did not say a word in answer to her. His disciples came and asked him, "Send her away, for she keeps calling out after us." He said in reply, "I was sent only to the lost sheep of the house of Israel." But the woman came and did him homage, saying, "Lord, help me." He said in reply, "It is not right to take the food of the children and throw it to the dogs." She said, "Please, Lord, for

> even the dogs eat the scraps that fall from
> the table of their masters." Then Jesus
> said to her in reply, "O woman, great
> is your faith! Let it be done for you as
> you wish." And her daughter was healed
> from that hour.

When you turn your heart to this gospel passage, opening your eyes and ears to the faith of this woman, you will learn how to pray. You can learn perseverance from her. There is no half love in her cry for help. She loves her wounded daughter. Even in the face of Jesus' seeming scorn, she pushes forward with an undivided heart. From her you can learn passion, confidence, and tenacity.

I like this woman. Her courage and boldness intrigue me. Her stubborn love captivates my heart. I need her steadfast faith. I would like to bring her single-hearted intention into all my prayer. She is one of my role models for prayer. I want to continue learning from her.

This woman teaches us that there is a spiritual power in us that can assist Jesus in answering prayer. Our love united with the love of Christ can wash over the one for whom we are praying and bring about healing. Perhaps God needs and desires our presence in order to work miracles of grace in the lives of those for whom we are praying.

Each day this week choose one person you know who is in need of healing. Go to Jesus with the determination and steadfast spirit of this woman. Lovingly insist that the healing take place. Then trust that it has.

O Healer of broken lives,

Gift me with the resilient spirit of this gospel woman. I need her willpower and self-assurance. Let me experience her love and passion, her undivided heart. I want to believe as she believed. Robe me with her faith. May her resilience flow over me!

Your teacher for this week is *the Canaanite woman* of this gospel. Look at her with penetrating eyes. Is there anything you want as much as she wanted healing for her daughter? Make a small list of things

you need to pray for; then go to Jesus with her faith.
How can she become your teacher?

> Resiliency is rooted in the human heart.
> It is an essential catalyst for moving through
> painful and devastating experiences.
> Resiliency is about being down and out and
> springing back,
> being persistent in the face of defeat....
> It is hope that holds on in spite of overwhelming loss.
> It is unrelenting faith.
>
> —Joyce Rupp

WEEK **FIFTEEN**

Carefully read Matthew 19:16–22, opening your heart to Jesus' invitation.

> Now someone approached him and said, "Teacher, what good must I do to gain eternal life?" He answered him, "Why do you ask me about the good? There is only One who is good. If you wish to enter into life, keep the commandments." He asked him, "Which ones?" And Jesus replied, "'You shall not kill; you shall not commit adultery; you shall not steal; you shall not bear false witness; honor your father and your mother'; and 'you shall love your neighbor as yourself.'" The young man said to him, "All of these I have observed. What do I still lack?" Jesus said to him, "If you wish to be perfect, go, sell what you have

> and give to [the] poor, and you will have treasure in heaven. Then come, follow me." When the young man heard this statement, he went away sad, for he had many possessions.

It is easy for me to identify with the young man who eagerly approached Jesus, wanting to be part of his life. I do this every time I sit down to pray. I make known my desire to be transformed. I want my life to be aligned with the life of Christ. I want to surrender all that impedes my spiritual progress. Yet, at times, I rise from my prayer and go away disappointed because I am unable to surrender the things that block my ability to be a true disciple of Christ. Some of the things that stand in my way are *possessions*. Yes, even those of us who aren't materially wealthy by the world's standards quickly discover how easily our *stuff* can get in the way of authentic Christian living. Thus I can relate to the rich man's sadness.

A story from Anthony de Mello that massages my sadness is that of a man who approaches a hermit in the forest asking to see a precious stone that he carries in his knapsack. The old hermit shows the man a huge diamond and then asks if he wants it. Filled with outward joy, the man takes the diamond and rushes back to his little hut. The next morning, however, he returns the diamond, saying, "Here, take this back and give me instead whatever it is you possess that made it so easy for you to give this away."

When I read this story I found myself wishing I possessed the mysterious grace of the old hermit. The welcoming truth is that I already have the gift for which I long, just as the rich young man also had it. We walk away sad not because we don't possess the steadfastness of our original longing but because we do possess it; yet it is like a treasure hidden in our lives. To find it we must grow in wisdom and grace. We must mature. And we will.

Jesus,

Even though a desire to follow you—to join your band, to be your disciple—is very much a part of my life, all too often I walk away sad. I want so many things that need to be surrendered, and so I waver. I hesitate. Even as I walk away I sense your look of love following me. Give me the grace to be obedient to your invitation to surrender all that impedes my desire to be your disciple. O may it come to pass!

Your teacher for the week is *your reluctance to surrender*. What can you learn from your reluctance?

Only our minds stand between us and God.
Go out of your mind.
The air outside is fresh and wild.
There's more reality there, waiting to dance.
Change the mantra to—"What can I give" instead of
"I want."

–Tom Bender

WEEK **SIXTEEN**

Read Luke 10:1–9 with a heart full of trust.

> After this the Lord appointed seventy[-two] others whom he sent ahead of him in pairs to every town and place he intended to visit. He said to them, "The harvest is abundant but the laborers are few; so ask the master of the harvest to send out laborers for his harvest. Go on your way; behold, I am sending you like lambs among wolves. Carry no money bag, no sack, no sandals; and greet no one along the way. Into whatever house you enter, first say, 'Peace to this household.' If a peaceful person lives there, your peace will rest on him; but if not, it will return to you. Stay in the same house and eat and drink what is offered to you, for the laborer deserves his

> payment. Do not move about from one
> house to another. Whatever town you
> enter and they welcome you, eat what
> is set before you, cure the sick in it and
> say to them, 'The kingdom of God is at
> hand for you.'"

When you go forth to bring the Word of God to others, take nothing with you except the guidance of the angels. Never forget that the heart of this command to go forth with *nothing* is trust. Trust God—you will be protected. Trust yourself—you will be amazed at your natural resources. Open your heart before you open your mouth. What you need to say will be revealed. And finally, trust those you are serving. There is a great hunger in people's hearts. God will provide the right word to touch that hunger. Your task is to trust.

As you journey forward to bring the Good News to others, it is the gold of trust you are to take with you. When you go forth with the jewel of God's Word, forget all the baggage you'd like to drag along. That baggage is control. It is fear. It is doubt. It is a little too much dependence on yourself. Leave all that behind. You are to go forth clothed in confidence. Utter dependence on God is the garment you are to wear. It will not be easy; yet when you learn how to travel lightly, you will find the peace for which you long.

Take some time this week to seriously consider what it means to travel lightly and to travel with trust. It may be helpful to record in your journal any issues you have with trust. Whom do you trust? Whom do you not trust? How can you trust a God you cannot see?

O God of all my journeys,

If you were checking my baggage when I leave for a trip, I wonder what you might take out and what you might put in. Make me a wise traveler. Teach me the art of traveling light. Reveal to me the natural resources of my life, those things I cannot put into a suitcase yet carry within me. Jesus, make known to me the path of life that I must walk. You are my power. You are my walking staff. If I travel with this attitude, my path is strewn with grace. O let it be so.

Your teacher for this week is *utter dependence on God*. Trust is necessary as you set up a partnership with this teacher.

You were born prepacked.
God looked at your entire life,
determined your assignment,
and gave you the tools to do the job.

–Max Lucado

WEEK **SEVENTEEN**

As you read Acts 20:28–38, try to experience the sentiments of Paul's disciples.

> "Keep watch over yourselves and over the whole flock of which the holy Spirit has appointed you overseers, in which you tend the church of God that he acquired with his own blood. I know that after my departure savage wolves will come among you, and they will not spare the flock. And from your own group, men will come forward perverting the truth to draw the disciples away after them. So be vigilant and remember that for three years, night and day, I unceasingly admonished each of you with tears. And now I commend you to God and to that gracious word of his that can build you up and give you the inheritance among

all who are consecrated. I have never wanted anyone's silver or gold or clothing. You know well that these very hands have served my needs and my companions. In every way I have shown you that by hard work of that sort we must help the weak, and keep in mind the words of the Lord Jesus who himself said, 'It is more blessed to give than to receive.'"

When he had finished speaking he knelt down and prayed with them all. They were all weeping loudly as they threw their arms around Paul and kissed him, for they were deeply distressed that he had said that they would never see his face again. Then they escorted him to the ship.

This tender scene reads like a beautiful painting. View it with your heart's eye: Paul, kneeling in prayer. His disciples gathered round, embracing him and anointing him with tears. What a convincing image of how much Paul was loved as a teacher of the Word! This remarkable testimony proclaims that his disciples had been deeply nourished by the spiritual food of Paul's message.

Paul's concern is almost tangible. His parting advice is also for us who are still moved by his words. We are to be vigilant, keeping tender watch over the Church. We are to guard the truth from those who would pervert it. There is no doubt that troubles will descend upon us, but let us be comforted anew in the way Paul tries to build up our faith.

In parting, he lovingly hands us over to God, reminding us of Jesus' words, "It is more blessed to give than to receive." He hands us over to the Christ of faith, that One whom we cannot see with human eyes yet in whose presence we walk all the days of our lives.

Paul, beloved teacher,

Intercede for us to God. The Church you left in our care needs support, healing, and encouragement. Give us words that will bring life to the People of God. Give us the kind of love that you portrayed in your parting gift to us. May your faith continue to light the embers of our lives, that we, too, might become flame! Let us be your torch.

Your teacher for this week is *the apostle Paul.* Choose one of his letters from scripture, and spend time with it this week. As you read his words, try to sense his love for Christ.

> Yet whatever gains I had,
> these I have come to regard as loss because of Christ.
> More than that, I regard everything as loss
> because of the surpassing value
> of knowing Christ Jesus my Lord.
> For his sake I have suffered the loss of all things,
> and I regard them as rubbish,
> in order that I may gain Christ and be found in him.
> –Philippians 3:7–8

WEEK **EIGHTEEN**

Read Job 3:1–3, 11–17, and 20–23 aloud, and try to experience Job's angst.

> After this, Job opened his mouth and
>   cursed his day. Job spoke out
>   and said:
> Perish the day on which I was born,
>   the night when they said, "The
>   child is a boy!" . . .
>
> Why did I not die at birth,
>   come forth from the womb and
>   expire?
> Why did knees receive me,
>   or breasts nurse me?
> For then I should have lain down and
>   been tranquil;
>   had I slept, I should then have
>   been at rest
> With kings and counselors of the earth

who rebuilt what were ruins
Or with princes who had gold
and filled their houses with silver.
Or why was I not buried away like a
stillborn child,
like babies that have never seen
the light?
There the wicked cease from troubling,
there the weary are at rest. . . .
Why is light given to the toilers,
life to the bitter in spirit?
They wait for death and it does not
come;
they search for it more than for
hidden treasures.
They rejoice in it exultingly,
and are glad when they find the
grave:
A man whose path is hidden from
him,
one whom God has hemmed in!

In one of his poems, Thomas Merton hints at the
truth that everyone has the right to have a bad day
once in a while. Well now, it appears that Job is having a very bad day, and I totally support him in his

need to lament. We all know a piece of Job's story: his prosperity, his loss, his misery, his acceptance, and his restoration.

What about us? What do we do when misery visits us? Perhaps we have been taught to be docile and humble when hard times come. Certainly there is a time for docility and acceptance. However, if we have not already learned this, we need to know that the friends of God find blessing in shouting out their misery. Isn't this what the psalmist teaches us? Take a look at Psalm 109. If we are friends of God, a reasonable amount of lamenting can be healthy, bringing us to a kind of deliverance from our turmoil. A day of lamentation can be good for the soul. You are being given permission to wail a bit. Have a good week of lamenting, if you need it, but do try not to make anyone else miserable.

Jesus,

You, too, experienced desolation and rejection; you understand Job's misery just as you understand ours. It is comforting to know that you listen to all the cries of our hearts, even when

*our cries are filled with agony and lament. Thank
you for your listening ear and open heart.*

Your teacher for this week is *your misery*. Surely you
will be able to find a few woes within your reach.
What can they teach you?

> Even though Job asked God to wipe the day
> of his birth off the calendar (Job 3:3–6),
> the days of pain exist
> right there along with the days of joy,
> and we are better off to face them.
>
> –Irene Nowell

WEEK **NINETEEN**

Read Ephesians 1:15–23, asking that this prayer come true in your life.

> Therefore, I, too, hearing of your faith in the Lord Jesus and of your love for all the holy ones, do not cease giving thanks for you, remembering you in my prayers, that the God of our Lord Jesus Christ, the Father of glory, may give you a spirit of wisdom and revelation resulting in knowledge of him. May the eyes of [your] hearts be enlightened, that you may know what is the hope that belongs to his call, what are the riches of glory in his inheritance among the holy ones, and what is the surpassing greatness of his power for us who believe, in accord with the exercise of his great might, which he worked in Christ, raising him from the

> dead and seating him at his right hand
> in the heavens, far above every principal-
> ity, authority, power, and dominion, and
> every name that is named not only in
> this age but also in the one to come. And
> he put all things beneath his feet and
> gave him as head over all things to the
> church, which is his body, the fullness of
> the one who fills all things in every way.

In the Rule of St. Benedict, monastics are asked to listen with the *ear of the heart*. In this beauti-ful prayer for the church at Ephesus, which can be a prayer for each of us, Paul prays that the *eyes of our hearts* be enlightened. In using descriptive and poetic language that depicts the heart having an ear and an eye, he implies a significant truth about the human person. We carry within us an immense potential for knowing God. We have been blessed with an inner vision that can assist us in discerning the divine mysteries hidden in our seemingly earth-bound hearts. If we learn the art of deep listening, we can hear the voice of God. Living like this, of course, requires a discipline that can only come from the grace of the Eternal One shaping our hearts.

Paul asks for the grace that each of us may inherit a portion of the wisdom and knowledge of God. In his renowned priestly prayer, Jesus prayed that we would all be one, united in faith, hope, and love: "Sanctify them in truth, your word is truth" (Jn 17:17, NRSV). In Paul's prayer for the Church, he is echoing that prayer of Jesus.

We pray that we may be given faith to comprehend the magnificence of God's power abiding in us. As we struggle through each day in these fragile bodies, it is consoling and frightening, attractive and overwhelming, to be reminded that the power of God in us is an invitation to be vibrant and dynamic. We are the caretakers of God's power in our world today. May our faithfulness rise up to embrace the challenge.

O Teacher of us all, in faith, I pray:

May the eyes of my heart be enlightened. May the ears of my heart listen to the good news of your indwelling presence in my life. With fierce love I commit myself to consciously carry your divine power in my being throughout this week. Do not allow me to set up obstacles to this gift of God in me. May the eyes and ears of my heart lead me to understand your power dwelling in me. May this come to pass!

Your teacher for the week will be *the eyes and ears of your heart*. What will your eyes and ears see and hear that will nurture your desire to learn?

> There is a time to listen to the whole
> and a time to listen to the part,
> a time to listen for how things go together
> and a time to shut out everything so we can hear
> what lives beneath our masks
>
> —Mark Nepo

WEEK **TWENTY**

Read Luke 15:11–32. Try to identify with each character in the story.

> Then Jesus said, "A man had two sons, and the younger son said to his father, 'Father, give me the share of your estate that should come to me.' So the father divided the property between them. After a few days, the younger son collected all his belongings and set off to a distant country where he squandered his inheritance on a life of dissipation. When he had freely spent everything, a severe famine struck that country, and he found himself in dire need. So he hired himself out to one of the local citizens who sent him to his farm to tend the swine. And he longed to eat his fill of the pods on which the swine fed, but

nobody gave him any. Coming to his senses he thought, 'How many of my father's hired workers have more than enough food to eat, but here am I, dying from hunger. I shall get up and go to my father and I shall say to him, "Father, I have sinned against heaven and against you. I no longer deserve to be called your son; treat me as you would treat one of your hired workers."' So he got up and went back to his father. While he was still a long way off, his father caught sight of him, and was filled with compassion. He ran to his son, embraced him and kissed him. His son said to him, 'Father, I have sinned against heaven and against you; I no longer deserve to be called your son.' But his father ordered his servants, 'Quickly bring the finest robe and put it on him; put a ring on his finger and sandals on his feet. Take the fattened calf and slaughter it. Then let us celebrate with a feast, because this son of mine was dead, and has come to life again; he was lost, and has been found.'

Then the celebration began. Now the older son had been out in the field and, on his way back, as he neared the house, he heard the sound of music and dancing. He called one of the servants and asked what this might mean. The servant said to him, 'Your brother has returned and your father has slaughtered the fattened calf because he has him back safe and sound.' He became angry, and when he refused to enter the house, his father came out and pleaded with him. He said to his father in reply, 'Look, all these years I served you and not once did I disobey your orders; yet you never gave me even a young goat to feast on with my friends. But when your son returns who swallowed up your property with prostitutes, for him you slaughter the fattened calf.' He said to him, 'My son, you are here with me always; everything I have is yours. But now we must celebrate and rejoice, because your brother was dead and has come to life again; he was lost and has been found.'"

It's my guess that I'm not alone when I confess I often feel like the prodigal son's older brother. I totally understand his sentiments. He was not able to rejoice over another's good fortune, because he was focusing on whether the recipient of his father's love was worthy of that love and forgiveness. He was also wallowing in his own imagined neglect: *I've been faithful all these years, and no one even noticed.* This gospel passage offers each of us marvelous material for prayer and reflection. Are we able to rejoice with another because of a good gift they've received, whether it is a material gift, a promotion or new opportunity, an affirmation, or a reward? Or has our fountain of joy dried up because we are floundering in our own misery?

Let this be a week of prayerful evaluation for you. Gaze into your heart to see if there may be a bit of rejoicing you are withholding. Practice being glad because of another's good fortune. Make an effort this week to affirm someone for something good that has happened to them.

O most merciful One,
    Encourage me to throw a party for the unwor-thy, knowing that I may be the guest of honor. Teach me to be joyful because of another person's good fortune even if I am feeling neglected. Let the party begin!

Your teacher for this week is *joy in another person's good fortune.* Be lavish in offering affirmation to others this week.

One of the sanest, surest,
and most generous joys of life
comes from being happy
over the good fortune of others.

–Archibald Rutledge

WEEK **TWENTY-ONE**

Prayerfully read Hosea 6:1–3. Read a second time and change the pronoun "us" to "me."

> Come, let us return to the LORD,
> For it is he who has torn, but he will heal
> us;
> he has struck down, but he will bind
> our wounds.
> He will revive us after two days;
> on the third day he will raise us up,
> to live in his presence.
> Let us know, let us strive to know the
> LORD;
> as certain as the dawn is his coming.
> He will come to us like the rain,
> like spring rain that waters the earth.

Living in the presence of God, with awareness, is a challenging piece of spiritual work. When the prophet tells us that God's coming is as certain as the dawn, we may be inclined to raise an eyebrow. Many of us do not experience that kind of certainty. That is why the sage advice "Strive to know the Lord" is necessary. The art of coming to know God is not without struggle.

We go to our place of prayer. Light a candle. Open the Bible. Burn some incense. Not one of these little rituals makes God present. God is already there. We may be the ones who need to discern the quality of our presence. It is not our rituals that are needed; it's our love and our full presence. "Come, let us return to the Lord," the prophet invites us. This week, let's try to put all our props away and return to God with our love—poor as it may be. The poverty of our love will raise us up to live in his presence.

God's coming is as certain as the dawn, we are told, but only if we have faith enough to wait in the darkness. Before we can live in certainty, we must learn to embrace uncertainty with the strong arms of faith. Faithfulness is more important than certainty. As we wait for the dawn with hope, are we able to trust the truth that God is already raising us up to live in his presence?

O dawning Presence,

As certain as the dawn is your coming, and so I will wait. I wait for you, O Lord. Waiting has never been easy for me, yet desire for you insists that I wait in expectancy. Transform my waiting into a prayer of confidence—a prayer of obedient hope. I wait for you, O Lord, like sentinels wait for the dawn. O dawning Presence, show me your face. Shine on me so that I, too, may be a new dawn. O let it be.

Your teacher for this week is *waiting for God*. Practice waiting each day. Ask yourself in prayer what you should wait for today. How can waiting be your teacher?

Those who wait for the LORD
shall renew their strength,
they shall mount up with wings like eagles,

they shall run and not be weary;
they shall walk and not faint.

–Isaiah 40:31 (NRSV)

WEEK **TWENTY-TWO**

Prayerfully read John 5:31–40, yearning to know the God of life.

> [Jesus said,] "If I testify on my own behalf, my testimony cannot be verified. But there is another who testifies on my behalf, and I know that the testimony he gives on my behalf is true. You sent emissaries to John, and he testified to the truth. I do not accept testimony from a human being, but I say this so that you may be saved. He was a burning and shining lamp, and for a while you were content to rejoice in his light. But I have testimony greater than John's. The works that the Father gave me to accomplish, these works that I perform testify on my behalf that the Father has sent me. Moreover, the Father who sent me

has testified on my behalf. But you have never heard his voice nor seen his form, and you do not have his word remaining in you, because you do not believe in the one whom he has sent. You search the scriptures, because you think you have eternal life through them; even they testify on my behalf. But you do not want to come to me to have life."

Many of us would suppose that in searching the scriptures we are, indeed, searching for God. In addressing his opponents in this week's gospel reading, Jesus implies that reading the scriptures and actually turning to him to possess eternal life are not necessarily the same. It is possible to study the scriptures for the wrong reasons. Perhaps we do this because it is the socially acceptable thing for a religious person to do. Or maybe we are trying to prove a point—going to the scriptures to make our case.

Sometimes we go to the scriptures to receive the comfort we need for daily life. Coming to Jesus for life suggests something even deeper than going to Jesus for comfort. It means we are completely open to being transformed and changed by the words we read. It means we wholeheartedly believe that Jesus *is* the Word made flesh. It means that we desire to be thoroughly transformed by the Word. Coming to Jesus for life requires climbing out of our comfort zones to the point of being willing to die in order to live. Are you there yet?

O Word of God,

Come alive in the pages of our hearts. Let your words flow out of the Book of Life and become flesh in our lives. Teach us to use the scripture as food for our souls and never as a weapon to defend our point of view. We turn to you for life. Receive us.

Your teacher for this week is *your desire for God*. Keep company with this desire.

Jesus has to be and become
ever more the center of my life.
It is not enough that Jesus is my teacher,

my guide, my source of inspiration.
It is not even enough
that he is my companion on the journey,
my friend and my brother.
Jesus must become the heart of my heart,
the fire of my life,
the love of my soul,
the bridegroom of my spirit.
He must become my only thought,
my only concern, my only desire.

–Henri Nouwen

WEEK **TWENTY-THREE**

Read Matthew 28:8–15 as though you were one of the Easter disciples.

> Then [the women] went away quickly from the tomb, fearful yet overjoyed, and ran to announce this to his disciples. And behold, Jesus met them on their way and greeted them. They approached, embraced his feet, and did him homage. Then Jesus said to them, "Do not be afraid. Go tell my brothers to go to Galilee, and there they will see me."
>
> While they were going, some of the guard went into the city and told the chief priests all that had happened. They assembled with the elders and took counsel; then they gave a large sum of money to the soldiers, telling them, "You are to say, 'His disciples came by night and stole

> him while we were asleep.' And if this gets
> to the ears of the governor, we will satisfy
> [him] and keep you out of trouble." The
> soldiers took the money and did as they
> were instructed. And this story has circu-
> lated among the Jews to the present [day].

"Fearful yet overjoyed"! It sounds as if these women
didn't know what to feel. They were beside themselves, as we sometimes say. They were taken by surprise. They couldn't believe their eyes. Perhaps they
were in-between believing and not believing. Their
mixture of joy and fear is understandable. It isn't
every morning that one experiences earthquakes and
angels rolling away stones from tombs—and finally
Jesus himself standing before you *alive*.

You and I have heard the Good News of Jesus'
resurrection in a little less dramatic manner: words
from the scriptures, a proclamation in our churches,
an alleluia sung after a long Lenten silence. Yet even
without the fanfare of a personal visitation, we sense
the necessary joy that hovers around this miracle of
life. Jesus is alive! Bring in the joy!

Will you choose joy rather than fear? The women in the gospel chose joy. No matter what season you are in when you meditate on the joy of these women disciples, allow this week to be a resurrection experience. Perhaps this will be the week when something in the womb of your heart will crack open with exuberance. You will lose your fear and allow the joy of your transformed life to overflow into your daily living.

Dear women at the tomb,

Intercede for me this week. I, too, would like to be a disciple of joy. Open my eyes to the moments of resurrection that surround me every day. There is always something rising, opening to new life, budding and blossoming, forgiving and transforming. Teach me to live awake that I may recognize the renaissance being celebrated in my midst at every moment. Make me a disciple of joy. Amen.

Your teacher for the week will be the *resurrection moments of each day*. Look for them daily. Claim them. Let there be joy!

There are empty tombs in all our lives still,
places where death did not conquer us
because faith entered in to fill the dark spots.
We have each risen from the dead
and Christ has risen in us.
Yes, the Easter season is about more than the
Resurrection of Jesus.
It is just as much about the resurrection
of everyone around Him because of His own.
Mary Magdalene rose again, this time a disciple.
The apostles rose again,
this time with courage and purpose.
The little people for whom Jesus' whole ministry
had been spent rose again,
this time with new conviction and certainty.
Rising again is the central message of the
Christian tradition.

–Joan Chittister

WEEK **TWENTY-FOUR**

Prayerfully read John 13:12–20. Listen to the anguish in Jesus' voice.

> So when he had washed their feet [and] put his garments back on and reclined at table again, [Jesus] said to them, "Do you realize what I have done for you? You call me 'teacher' and 'master,' and rightly so, for indeed I am. If I, therefore, the master and teacher, have washed your feet, you ought to wash one another's feet. I have given you a model to follow, so that as I have done for you, you should also do. Amen, amen, I say to you, no slave is greater than his master nor any messenger greater than the one who sent him. If you understand this, blessed are you if you do it. I am not speaking of all of you. I know those whom I have chosen.

But so that the scripture might be fulfilled, 'The one who ate my food has
raised his heel against me.' From now
on I am telling you before it happens,
so that when it happens you may believe
that I AM. Amen, amen, I say to you,
whoever receives the one I send receives
me, and whoever receives me receives the
one who sent me."

This tender moment of Jesus washing his apostles'
feet turns bittersweet when we hear him emphasiz-
ing the sad truth that one who broke bread with
him turned against him. Jesus could also claim that
someone whose feet he just washed turned against
him. What went wrong? Why such betrayal?

Jesus chose his apostles just as, in some unique
way, he chooses us. When he chooses us to be his
disciples, he calls each of us to be a foot-washer and
a bread-breaker in daily life. Has it ever occurred to
you that the people who surround you have, in some
way, been sent to you by God? They have been chosen, and you have been chosen to circle through one
another's lives as a welcoming presence, a constant

blessing. Foot-washing and bread-breaking are metaphors for the ministry that takes place in our lives. When you minister to one another, you are ministering to Christ. Do you recognize the daily ministry that goes on in your own household of faith? You may not betray one another as Jesus was betrayed, but how often do you take one another for granted? What goes wrong? Why this betrayal?

Take some time this week to pray for the people in your life whom you may have taken for granted, which in a sense is a small betrayal. In your journal, inscribe the names of specific persons. Look at each person on your list with love. Say aloud to each one, *When I come into your presence, it is like coming into the presence of God.* These words may be difficult to swallow; however, if you pray these words often, your attitude about some people may undergo a profound change.

Jesus, our servant king,
*   You have placed in our lives disciples of your own heart for us to love. Shine your light into our lives, that we might see more clearly the little*

*ways we betray one another. Make of us a peren-
nial presence, a beautiful blessing, a sacramental
sign of your love for those you have bequeathed
to us. May we never take each other for granted.*

Your teachers for this week will be *those whom God
has chosen to be a part of your life*: family, coworkers,
community members, and others.

One of the most heartrending stories
of forgiveness after betrayal
takes place between Jacob and Esau.
Years after Esau's blessing was stolen,
the two brothers are about to meet again.
Jacob approaches Esau with trepidation
not knowing what to expect.
When it becomes obvious
that his brother's heart is not embittered
Jacob speaks words that can only be the Word of God:
*To come into your presence is like
coming into the presence of God
now that you have received me so kindly.*
                    –Macrina Wiederkehr, based on Genesis 33

WEEK **TWENTY-FIVE**

Prayerfully read Luke 9:1–6 with an openness to receiving the grace you need for your ministry.

> [Jesus] summoned the Twelve and gave them power and authority over all demons and to cure diseases, and he sent them to proclaim the kingdom of God and to heal [the sick]. He said to them, "Take nothing for the journey, neither walking stick, nor sack, nor food, nor money, and let no one take a second tunic. Whatever house you enter, stay there and leave from there. And as for those who do not welcome you, when you leave that town, shake the dust from your feet in testimony against them." Then they set out and went from village to village proclaiming the good news and curing diseases everywhere.

The very first fragment of this gospel's sentence—"[Jesus] summoned the Twelve and gave them power"—took my breath away, and so I stopped for reflection before finishing the sentence. As I put myself in the company of the twelve disciples, I want to believe these words are meant for all of us. We have all been summoned by Christ. We, too, are anointed ones who have been given power.

Let this be the heart of your prayer this week. You have been summoned and given power. The power you are given is Christ Power. That is why Jesus explains to the disciples that when they go forth to heal and teach it is unnecessary to take a lot of stuff along. "Take nothing on your journey," Jesus says. The power he has bequeathed to them is quite enough. The resources they need, they already possess. Perhaps we, too, can practice believing that.

It is not easy to believe that we have enough resources to be disciples of Jesus. It is not easy to believe that if we are followers of Jesus, we have a power that has been handed down to us. It is not like the power of the mighty ones of this world. It is a power that empowers us to be another Christ in this world.

Jesus,

You are my power and my grace. You are my walking staff and my lamp. You are the only resource I need. Your power is enough for me. When I falter, craving a more exciting and worldly power, look at me with eyes of acceptance. Forgive me and lift me up again into the arms of grace. Put your staff in my hand as I go forth to live the gospel of my life. Amen.

Your teacher this week is *the gift of simplicity.* To be a vessel of healing for others, all you need is your life, Jesus says. Practice simplicity this week. Listen to your best self. All you need is your emptied-out self. Let go of the add-ons.

> One of the hardest things to do in letting go
> is giving up the need to be something.
>   –Richard Rohr

WEEK **TWENTY-SIX**

As you read John 20:19–23, open your heart to the breath of the Spirit.

> On the evening of that first day of the week, when the doors were locked, where the disciples were, for fear of the Jews, Jesus came and stood in their midst and said to them, "Peace be with you." When he had said this, he showed them his hands and his side. The disciples rejoiced when they saw the Lord. [Jesus] said to them again, "Peace be with you. As the Father has sent me, so I send you." And when he had said this, he breathed on them and said to them, "Receive the holy Spirit. Whose sins you forgive are forgiven them, and whose sins you retain are retained."

The doors were locked, and the disciples' hearts were fearful. Fearful hearts are locked hearts. Locked doors and locked hearts, however, were not strong enough to prevent Jesus from breaking into their lives. Love broke in. Jesus breathed on his friends, giving them the first fruits of the Spirit.

Later, on that first Pentecost Day, still lacking in power but full of hope, these same disciples, and probably more, waited for the promise to be fulfilled—the promise of receiving the fullness of the Spirit (see Acts 1:4). The fact that they were waiting together says much about the importance of community. With fragile hope they waited. Suddenly the joyful, awesome sound of wind and fire arrived. Fearful hearts blossomed with courage and were transformed. Barriers that came from not understanding one another were burned away with the fire of the Spirit.

In that moment the disciples must have remembered their personal prelude to the great Pentecost when Jesus came through locked doors and breathed on them. In the mystery of eternity, you and I were present also. Whatever challenges you may face on your path of life, open yourself relentlessly to the breath of the Spirit.

O Breath of God,

Blow gently on the gifts that have weakened or grown stale in my life. Stir up the flame of my original love, faith, and hope. Open my locked doors, and breathe on me anew. May my own fearful heart blossom with courage as I begin this new week. O Breath of God, may a new Pentecost take place in my life!

Your teacher for this week is *the Holy Spirit*. Allow the Spirit to teach you. Listen to the movement of the Spirit in your daily life. The Spirit is the love between Jesus and the Father overflowing and spilling out on you.

The affection between Son and Father
is so utterly alive
as to be not merely a bond but another person,
the Holy Spirit.

That constant, passionate spill-over of pure affection
is the Spirit.
This is the Spirit of affection in which
we live and move in every moment
and it is at the heart of the Christian notion of God.

                              —John O'Donohue

WEEK **TWENTY-SEVEN**

Read Psalm 33:8–15, 20–22, with delight at the thought of being chosen by God.

> Let all the earth fear the LORD;
>> let all who dwell in the world show
>>> him reverence.
> For he spoke, and it came to be,
>> commanded, and it stood in place.
> The LORD foils the plan of nations,
>> frustrates the designs of peoples.
> But the plan of the LORD stands forever,
>> the designs of his heart through all
>>> generations.
> Blessed is the nation whose God is the
>> LORD,
>> the people chosen as his inheritance.
>
> From heaven the LORD looks down
>> and observes the children of Adam,
> From his dwelling place he surveys

all who dwell on earth.
The One who fashioned together their
hearts
is the One who knows all their
works. . . .

Our soul waits for the LORD,
he is our help and shield.
For in him our hearts rejoice;
in his holy name we trust.
May your mercy, LORD, be upon us;
as we put our hope in you.

To believe that God has chosen us as his inheritance is mind-bending. Sometimes we just mouth the psalms and fail to consciously consider what is being said. Knowing how much discord often arises when trying to divide up inheritance, it would serve us well to meditate on these enriching words: "Blessed is the nation whose God is the LORD, the people chosen as his inheritance" (v. 12). As you read through this psalm, try to get a sense of how the psalmist sees the world filled with the mercy of God. Perhaps it is the mercy of God that is our inheritance. To have a share in the benevolence of

God is, indeed, a gift. Repeat the following sentence a number of times: "I have inherited the mercy of God."

If this knowledge could reach the inner core of our being, perhaps our fighting over possessions, land, and money would cease. We would then discover our true inheritance in the love and kindness we've inherited from our Creator. You may be thinking, *You are talking to the wind. Look at the greed of the peoples of this world. This is not going to change.* And you are right. It is not going to change unless we change it together. So let's dream!

What might our lives be like if the inheritance we would recognize and claim as our own would be the mercy of God? What if families, communities, and nations would acknowledge that our greatest inheritance is the gift of one another? What if we would choose each other as our inheritance? What if we would believe that, as the text above implies, in some imperceptible way God has chosen us as his inheritance? What then? What would our lives be like? I think I know the answer to those questions. Do you?

O God of the nations,

In your loving kindness, transform us into neighbors instead of nations. Take the kindness and mercy of a few people to your heart and breathe on it. Increase that mercy, and make it contagious so that the world will be filled with people who care for each other. O God of the ages, you have worked many miracles in the past. Work them again in our day. O may it come to pass!

Your teacher for this week is *mercy*. Look for it everywhere: in yourself, in others, and in nature. Try to be aware of how *your* mercy flows out of your awareness of God's mercy.

I have always found
that mercy bears richer fruits
than strict justice.

—Abraham Lincoln

WEEK **TWENTY-EIGHT**

Read Psalm 18:2–4, allowing new names for God to rise out of your heart and from your lips.

> I love you, LORD, my strength,
> > LORD, my rock, my fortress, my deliverer,
>
> My God, my rock of refuge,
> > my shield, my saving horn, my stronghold!
>
> Praised be the LORD, I exclaim!
> > I have been delivered from my enemies.

Sometimes in the midst of a crisis it is comforting to call God by names that reveal why we are lifting up our hearts and asking for divine assistance. To claim that God is a rock of refuge and a shield suggests that we need a safe place to turn for protection. What names do you have for that safe place where you go in times of trouble? At this particular season in your life, what new names are flowing out of your relationship with God? What descriptive images best illustrate your encounter with the Divine?

God as a refuge and shield for us is a frequent theme in the psalms. Yet no matter how rich these scriptural themes may be, we must ask how these words become flesh in our lives. How do we get the words off the page and into our hearts? It requires more than just saying, "God, you are my refuge," to actually experience God as refuge. It entails more than reciting beautiful phrases to have a felt sense of God being a protective shield in our lives. It requires unrelenting practice to remember the ever-present nature of the Holy One in whom we live and move and have our being.

In your prayer this week, open your heart to fresh images of God. How has God been a listening presence for you? Are you able to perceive God as a soul-friend and beloved companion? Have you experienced a surge of living water moving through your being? Is God your shepherd, your pearl of great price? Is God your poem and your song? Is God your rock?

O God beyond all names,
I want to encounter the unfathomable poem
that you are. O Holy One, you have pitched a tent
in my heart. You are my shelter, my tree of life.
You are my cave, my haven, my abode. You are
the sanctuary where I dwell. I am the sanctuary
where you dwell. I do not ask you to free me
from the storms of life that assist my growth. I
ask only that you protect me and help me make
wise choices. O let it be!

Choose *a name that flows out of your relationship with God*, and let that name be your teacher this week (e.g., Sheltering Tree, Graceful Presence, Rock of Ages, etc.).

> Cave of Refuge, provide a sanctuary of solace
> as I wait for the unrecognizable future to reveal itself.
> Do not let my troubles steal my joy.
>
> —Joyce Rupp

WEEK **TWENTY-NINE**

Prayerfully read Matthew 9:27–31. Where are the places in your life where you need both sight and insight?

> And as Jesus passed on from there, two blind men followed [him], crying out, "Son of David, have pity on us!" When he entered the house, the blind men approached him and Jesus said to them, "Do you believe that I can do this?" "Yes, Lord," they said to him. Then he touched their eyes and said, "Let it be done for you according to your faith." And their eyes were opened. Jesus warned them sternly, "See that no one knows about this." But they went out and spread word of him through all that land.

Let's suppose that the two blind men of this gospel passage are actually only one person and that person is you. Or perhaps there are two blind spots in your life crying for your attention. These are places where you need to see more clearly.

The voice crying out for mercy is your voice. Spend a little time listening to your own voice asking Jesus for compassion and healing. Jesus then asks you to offer that same mercy to yourself. Observe your act of being merciful to yourself. What does that entail? Pause now and reflect on this. With the eyes of your heart, visualize your mercy flowing out of your brokenness into your places of greatest need.

Name two areas in your life where you detect there is blindness. Now imagine that Jesus has given you the power to do for yourself what he did for the blind ones in the gospel. Symbolically reach out and touch those blind places in your life. Envision yourself doing this. How can you offer compassion to yourself? Where are you in need of the grace of new sight? Do you have enough faith? Now, literally touch your eyes! When your eyes open, what will they see?

Jesus,

Sometimes I pray with the gospels, forgetting that these biblical characters can represent me. There are times when I am the one who needs to be fed, healed, and touched into wholeness. In today's gospel I put myself in the place of these two blind men. I want to experience what they felt when they asked to be healed. I want to know their joy in finally being able to see. I am grateful for the many ways you restore my sight each day! Increase my faith.

Your teacher for this week is *your own blindness.*

The only thing worse
than being blind
is having sight
but no vision.

–Helen Keller

WEEK **THIRTY**

Prayerfully read Matthew 8:18–22. In reading this text, ask yourself, "How is Jesus my teacher?"

> When Jesus saw a crowd around him, he gave orders to cross to the other side. A scribe approached and said to him, "Teacher, I will follow you wherever you go." Jesus answered him, "Foxes have dens and birds of the sky have nests, but the Son of Man has nowhere to rest his head." Another of [his] disciples said to him, "Lord, let me go first and bury my father." But Jesus answered him, "Follow me, and let the dead bury their dead."

We don't know if the scribe who spoke these words was speaking as an eager disciple or as a cynical antagonist. The scribes of the synoptic gospels were not always friendly to Jesus or supportive of his mission. Regardless of the intent of the scribe, however, most of us can recognize these words as good content for the prayer of a disciple. If you would like to be a disciple of Jesus, cradle these words in your heart: "Teacher, I will follow you wherever you go." Each day this week, use these words as a mantra. Let them follow you through the week. As you abide in these words, note that Jesus lays down some difficult conditions for being a disciple.

Perhaps as we reverently break open the Word and unpack its meaning, we may discern that what Jesus is really saying is this: *If you want to be my disciple, you must learn the art of surrender. All your carefully laid-out agendas and your creative plans must be cast aside. Do not wait until, in your opinion, everything is in perfect order in your life. If you choose to keep company with one who had nowhere to lay his head, then you must be willing to live without certainty.*

O wise Teacher,
    If I want to be your disciple, I must follow you wherever you go. I know you are inviting me not

only to sit at your feet but also to get on the road with you. You speak words that shake me out of the lethargic rut of daily living. You walk roads that cause me to examine my timidity. Even if I seem reluctant to be your disciple, hopefully you will sense my shy yearning. Create in me a steadfast heart. Give me the wisdom and courage to follow your lead. Make my wish come true. Amen to being your disciple.

Your teacher for this week is *your hidden disciple*. How can you coax that cautious devotee out of hiding? How can you learn from the person you long to be?

There is something in you that is hidden.
It has always been there waiting,
waiting for you to believe in it,
waiting for you to invite it to be your daily companion,
waiting for you to embrace it rather than fear it.

It is courageous, wise, gentle and hopeful.
How about taking your hidden disciple for a
walk today?

—Macrina Wiederkehr

WEEK **THIRTY-ONE**

Prayerfully read Matthew 8:5–13. From what kind of paralysis do you need to be cured?

> When [Jesus] entered Capernaum, a centurion approached him and appealed to him, saying, "Lord, my servant is lying at home paralyzed, suffering dreadfully." He said to him, "I will come and cure him." The centurion said in reply, "Lord, I am not worthy to have you enter under my roof; only say the word and my servant will be healed. For I too am a person subject to authority, with soldiers subject to me. And I say to one, 'Go,' and he goes; and to another, 'Come here,' and he comes; and to my slave, 'Do this,' and he does it." When Jesus heard this, he was amazed and said to those following him, "Amen, I say to

you, in no one in Israel have I found such faith. I say to you, many will come from the east and the west, and will recline with Abraham, Isaac, and Jacob at the banquet in the kingdom of heaven, but the children of the kingdom will be driven out into the outer darkness, where there will be wailing and grinding of teeth." And Jesus said to the centurion, "You may go; as you have believed, let it be done for you." And at that very hour [his] servant was healed.

The words "I will come and cure him" are Jesus' generous offer to come to the centurion's house and heal his sick servant. Who among us would not open every door to receive Jesus into our homes? Thus the centurion's response may come as a surprise. With trust and faith he explains that it is not necessary for Jesus to come into his house. He understands what it is to have a busy schedule with many responsibilities. He knows what it is to be a person with authority and power. Moreover, he doesn't even feel worthy of the great honor of Jesus entering his house. "Only say the word and my servant will be healed," he pleads. Jesus is stunned at the faith the centurion displays. He respects his humble request and answers his prayer.

To cure the short supply of faith many of us have, I suggest the practice of prayerfully using the centurion's words when we ask a favor of God. Let us put on the robe of humility and trust as we, too, cry out in our need, "Only say the word and my prayer will be granted." Part of intercessory prayer is to practice believing that, in *God's* time, it shall be done. Practice this prayer right now. Think of something specific to ask of Jesus, and pray, "Only say the word and my request will be granted." Wait in silence, and trust that your cry to God will become an answered prayer.

Compassionate Healer,

There are places in my life where mending is needed. Throughout this week I will bring these broken places to you. Support me in my desire to be vulnerable. Each time I request healing for a weakness in my life I will use the centurion's prayer, "Only say the word and my request will be

*granted." Then I will be still and wait. I will listen
to you answering my prayer. Give me humility to
name my weakness. Give me faith to believe you
will hear me. Give me trust to wait in silence while
you are answering my prayer. Amen.*

Your teacher for this week will be *trust in prayer.*

> [Jesus] often retired alone
> and spent the night in silence and prayer.
> The fruit of silence is prayer,
> The fruit of prayer is faith,
> The fruit of faith is love,
> The fruit of love is service,
> The fruit of service is peace.
> Let us provide each other
> an atmosphere of peace and quiet
> which will facilitate prayer, work, study, and rest.
>
> —St. Teresa of Calcutta

WEEK **THIRTY-TWO**

Read Mark 10:35–45. At this season in your life, what is the cup of suffering you must drink?

> Then James and John, the sons of Zebedee, came to him and said to him, "Teacher, we want you to do for us whatever we ask of you." He replied, "What do you wish [me] to do for you?" They answered him, "Grant that in your glory we may sit one at your right and the other at your left." Jesus said to them, "You do not know what you are asking. Can you drink the cup that I drink or be baptized with the baptism with which I am baptized?" They said to him, "We can." Jesus said to them, "The cup that I drink, you will drink, and with the baptism with which I am baptized, you will be baptized; but to sit at my right or

at my left is not mine to give but is for those for whom it has been prepared." When the ten heard this, they became indignant at James and John. Jesus summoned them and said to them, "You know that those who are recognized as rulers over the Gentiles lord it over them, and their great ones make their authority over them felt. But it shall not be so among you. Rather, whoever wishes to be great among you will be your servant; whoever wishes to be first among you will be the slave of all. For the Son of Man did not come to be served but to serve and to give his life as a ransom for many."

What a charming and endearing human portrait is painted of James and John in this gospel! I can hear you wondering, *Charming? Endearing?* We may be inclined to smirk at their egotistical request. Before we begin to judge them too harshly for their desire to have first place in the reign of God, let's remember that these are two of the disciples Jesus chose to take with him to the mount of transfiguration.

Thus, even when we are individually chosen by Jesus, we are capable of having foolish dreams and missing the point of the radical nature of the Gospel. We may not proclaim that we want first place, yet how often do we find ourselves pushing to the front of the line?

As Christians we are called to serve. We are also called to drink of the cup from which Jesus drank. It is a cup of mystery; it is a cup of suffering. We never know how we will handle the cup until it is handed to us. When suffering comes into our lives in one of its many forms, we need to learn how to give it a home and to open ourselves to learn what it is able to teach us.

In my experience, this cup of suffering usually holds a hidden gift—an ambiguous grace. We may have to hold the cup longer than we wish in order to discern the hidden gift; however, holding the cup is crucial. Seldom is the gift visible as we drink. This is why reflection on the cup is essential.

O Comforter of troubled hearts,

Each life is a cup of suffering and a cup of joy. I am often tempted to turn from the cup of suffering, seeking only the cup of joy. Teach me to trust the cup of suffering. Strengthen me in my desire to hold this cup as long as needed. Assist me in finding grace in each sip. Support me in coming to understand the cup of suffering as an experienced teacher. Yes to the cup you offer!

Your teacher for this week is *the cup of suffering*. Linger with this cup in your hands. Name a particular suffering each day of this week. What can it teach you? How can it make you more sensitive to the sorrow of others?

The heart is stretched through suffering, and enlarged.
But O the agony of this enlarging of the heart,
that one may be prepared
to enter into the anguish of others.

–Thomas Kelly

WEEK **THIRTY-THREE**

As you read Matthew 6:7–15, pray the Lord's Prayer in a contemplative manner.

> [Jesus said,] "When you are praying, do not heap up empty phrases as the Gentiles do; for they think that they will be heard because of their many words. Do not be like them, for your Father knows what you need before you ask him.
>
> "Pray then in this way:

Our Father in heaven,
  hallowed be your name.
  Your kingdom come.
  Your will be done,
      on earth as it is in heaven.
  Give us this day our daily bread.
  And forgive us our debts,
      as we also have forgiven our
      debtors.

> And do not bring us to the time of
>   trial,
>   but rescue us from the evil one.
>
> "For if you forgive others their trespass-
> es, your heavenly Father will also forgive
> you; but if you do not forgive others,
> neither will your Father forgive your
> trespasses." (NRSV)

Many words do not necessarily make good prayer. God hears your prayer not because of your countless words but because of your love. This truth is suggested by Jesus just before he teaches his disciples the Lord's Prayer.

In our much-loved Lord's Prayer, it is the spirit of prayer that Jesus is trying to open our hearts to recognize and value. He is indirectly saying, "Don't try to get heaven's attention by a lot of wordy prayers." As a child seeks the comfort of a loving parent, let your needs be known. Heaven leans down and listens to the prayer of a humble spirit. The One to whom you pray is holy; remember the hallowedness of God's name. Pray that the reign of God may surround you during your sojourn on earth. Yearn to do God's will. Anticipate your daily bread with trust. Learn forgiveness. Pray to do good and not evil. Then will your heart be filled with the spirit of prayer.

It is not the words you pray that move God to listen to your prayer. God sees the love in your heart and is impelled to listen to your prayer. Words are the least important part of prayer.

O God of silence and of words,

You know our needs before we ask. You know our heart before we speak. You know our desires before we voice them. You know your plan for us. Perhaps this is why you caution us not to babble, prattle, chatter, and jabber in our prayer. You want our prayer to be simple: a cry of the heart, a yearning from the core of our being, a moment of trust in the darkness. You desire a prayer that is humble and unpretentious. You want us to be natural and down-to-earth. School us to know our true needs, that we may learn how to pray as you would have us pray. So be it!

Your teacher for the week will be *wordless prayer*. Focus on one phrase of the Lord's Prayer each day, and then move into the *prayer of being*.

> If God is the Center of your life,
> no words are necessary.
> Your mere presence will touch hearts.
>
> —St. Vincent de Paul

WEEK **THIRTY-FOUR**

Prayerfully read Mark 12:38–44. Pray for the grace of a pure heart and right intention.

> In the course of his teaching [Jesus] said, "Beware of the scribes, who like to go around in long robes and accept greetings in the marketplaces, seats of honor in synagogues, and places of honor at banquets. They devour the houses of widows and, as a pretext, recite lengthy prayers. They will receive a very severe condemnation."
>
> He sat down opposite the treasury and observed how the crowd put money into the treasury. Many rich people put in large sums. A poor widow also came and put in two small coins worth a few cents. Calling his disciples to himself, he said to them, "Amen, I say to you, this poor widow put

> in more than all the other contributors to
> the treasury. For they have all contributed
> from their surplus wealth, but she, from
> her poverty, has contributed all she had,
> her whole livelihood."

As you read this gospel, spend some time contemplating what Jesus is saying. The nucleus of his message seems to be that the good we do ought to flow from our hearts. It is possible to do good things for the wrong reasons. We can learn to guard our hearts and check our intentions. Why do we do the good that we do? Could we be searching for approval and affirmation from others? We who are created in God's image have been given hearts of compassion and love. These are gifts that our Creator gave us at the beginning of our lives, hoping that we might discover them before the end of our lives. How disappointing it would be to do good things with the wrong motives!

In his teaching Jesus admonishes those in positions of authority and power not to get stuck in petty, legalistic, external practices, forgetting the more authentic places of the heart. In his poem "The

Little Ways That Encourage Good Fortune," William Stafford sounds a bit like Jesus in cautioning folks who are trying to make things right in the lives of others yet do not have things right in their own lives. We might take that to heart for pondering.

In our reading for this week, Jesus holds up the poor widow as a shining light. She is a model for us. Her two small coins are symbols not of wealth and prestige but of immense love. She was not concerned about impressing anyone. She simply gave what she could from a pure heart. She was being obedient to love, and Jesus wants us to notice that: "Blessed are the pure of heart for they shall see God" (Mt 5:8). Perhaps we can take her as our spiritual guide this week as we, too, look for ways to be obedient to love.

Jesus, Guardian of my soul,

Help me be attentive to the motives behind my actions this week. Watch over my heart. Give me the pure heart of beatitude loving and living. Teach me to give my all not to be applauded but simply because your love in me cannot be contained. My love wants to flow forth as gift. O let it flow!

Your teacher for this week is *the widow of our gospel and her two small coins*. What can you learn from those two coins and her obedient love?

> I hold that Love, where present,
> cannot possibly be content
> with remaining always the same.
>
> —St. Teresa of Avila

WEEK **THIRTY-FIVE**

Prayerfully read Mark 7:31–37; then ask yourself, What kind of miracle do I need in order to hear and see more responsibly?

> Again [Jesus] left the district of Tyre and went by way of Sidon to the Sea of Galilee, into the district of the Decapolis. And people brought to him a deaf man who had a speech impediment and begged him to lay his hand on him. He took him off by himself away from the crowd. He put his finger into the man's ears and, spitting, touched his tongue; then he looked up to heaven and groaned, and said to him, "*Ephphatha!*" (that is, "Be opened!") And [immediately] the man's ears were opened, his speech impediment was removed, and he spoke plainly. He ordered them not

to tell anyone. But the more he ordered
them not to, the more they proclaimed
it. They were exceedingly astonished and
they said, "He has done all things well.
He makes the deaf hear and [the] mute
speak."

Have you ever wondered why Jesus looked toward
heaven and groaned before opening the deaf-mute's
ears and loosening his tongue? Why the groaning?
Sometimes we groan when we are weary, sad, or
concerned. Being commissioned to a task that
seems impossible may bring forth a groan. Being
bone-weary at the end of the day without much to
show for it may bring forth a groan. Beginning a
project that is of critical importance may evoke a
groan.

Jesus' mission sent him forth to heal. His gesture
of opening ears for hearing and freeing the tongue
for speaking was an act of obedience. Perhaps his
groaning was a holy sigh. Jesus was united to the
deaf-mute's anguish and to the One who had sent
him to heal. Open ears and a free tongue make one
accountable. What will happen to this child of God

who is being restored to health? Will those ears be used to listen to the cries of the poor? Will that tongue speak words of blessing and healing for others? Healing and being healed brings responsibility. To be united to God while praying for healing is crucial. In our daily prayer for renewal, perhaps we all need to look to the heavens and groan.

Jesus, Savior of the world,

I stand before the globe representing the nations of this world, and I groan. There is an anguish I experience as I consider the burdens of our world. Laying my hands on the globe, I ask for the healings I read about in the gospels. This globe represents people, animals, plants, trees, rivers, oceans, earth, and air. It is your gift to us, yet so often we are blind, deaf, and mute in relation to the needs of our planet. Hear this groan of anguish as we look to the heavens for support. Open the eyes of the peoples. Unstop their ears and give them voice. Let the healing begin!

Your teachers for the week are *the things you are reluctant to see and hear*. This is your week to look toward the heavens and groan. How can you learn from what ought not to be?

> Carry your lighted lamp quietly and steadily. . . .
> If you could for one hour be with your Divine Self
> you could change the mood of your surroundings,
> so powerful is this light. Try it!
> Hold the nations in the palm of your hand
> and shine on them.
>
> —Adapted from Mary Strong,
> *Letters of the Scattered
> Brotherhood*

WEEK **THIRTY-SIX**

Prayerfully read Luke 6:27–36 as you reflect on your incredible potential to love.

> [Jesus said,] "But to you who hear I say, love your enemies, do good to those who hate you, bless those who curse you, pray for those who mistreat you. To the person who strikes you on one cheek, offer the other one as well, and from the person who takes your cloak, do not withhold even your tunic. Give to everyone who asks of you, and from the one who takes what is yours do not demand it back. Do to others as you would have them do to you. For if you love those who love you, what credit is that to you? Even sinners love those who love them. And if you do good to those who do good to you, what credit is that to you?

Even sinners do the same. If you lend money to those from whom you expect repayment, what credit [is] that to you? Even sinners lend to sinners, and get back the same amount. But rather, love your enemies and do good to them, and lend expecting nothing back; then your reward will be great and you will be children of the Most High, for he himself is kind to the ungrateful and the wicked. Be merciful, just as [also] your Father is merciful."

Our reading for today is a good description of *tough love*. If we are to be followers of Jesus, we are to live out of the pure goodness of our hearts. We never count the cost of loving. When we do good deeds, we don't keep score of who deserves our kindness. We're not always checking our possessions to see if everything we loaned to another has been returned. The gifts we give are given freely. We do not give, expecting return payment. Judging and condemning others is simply not a part of our lifestyle. If someone takes something that is ours, let it go.

Ouch! Most of us have not yet learned to live with such radical abandon. Nevertheless, I suggest that we practice believing in our own goodness as we reread this passage. The difficult things we are asked to do can be carried out only if we have owned the truth that we belong to Christ, thus we are created to be lovers. When we are able to live out of the goodness implanted in us by God, our enemies can become people we sincerely care about. Loving is a choice. We have been asked to love one another unselfishly; however, we are never forced to love. Forced love is not love; it is fear. What can you learn from your potential to love?

O ancient Love,

My heart is just a muscle. It can't love, yet it sends blood, oxygen, and nutrients to all parts of my body by means of blood vessels. It keeps me alive. Sounds like love to me! I, too, am a vessel of love, a carrier of good to others. I can help keep others alive by sending the nutrients of hope, courage, and faith to them. O Lover of us all, your heart was broken open for us. Help us to believe in our own love, which is akin to your love for us. Teach us how to love in a world of fear. May love be born each day! Amen.

Be quiet for a few moments, and drink in the truth that you have been created to love. Your potential to love is vast. Your teacher for this week is, very simply, *the gift of your love*. What will you allow it to teach you?

> Love comes out of God and gathers us to God
> in order to pour itself back into God through all of us
> and bring us all back to Him
> on the tide of His own infinite mercy.
> So we all become doors and windows
> through which God shines back into His own house.
>
> —Thomas Merton

WEEK **THIRTY-SEVEN**

Prayerfully read Luke 8:43–48, keeping your eye on the hem of Jesus' garment.

> And a woman afflicted with hemorrhages for twelve years, who [had spent her whole livelihood on doctors and] was unable to be cured by anyone, came up behind him and touched the tassel on his cloak. Immediately her bleeding stopped. Jesus then asked, "Who touched me?" While all were denying it, Peter said, "Master, the crowds are pushing and pressing in upon you." But Jesus said, "Someone has touched me; for I know that power has gone out from me." When the woman realized that she had not escaped notice, she came forward trembling. Falling down before him, she explained in the presence of all

the people why she had touched him and
how she had been healed immediately.
He said to her, "Daughter, your faith has
saved you; go in peace."

Weary and desperate, she pushed through the crowd
searching for healing—the woman without a name.
Who is she? She could be anyone. She could be
you. Discouraged with the burdens of life and poor
health, she had her eye on Jesus. She settled for
touching the fringe of his garment, and although
that touch cost her dearly, it also blessed her with
the healing for which she was seeking. *Who touched
me?* Jesus asked. That costly touch took away her
privacy. She was singled out, and her faith became
public knowledge. Her intrusion into Jesus' space
made her vulnerable. *Power has gone out from me,*
Jesus said.

I admire this faith-filled woman who pushed
through the crowd seeking healing. Sometimes
when I search for the fringe of Jesus' garment, I
suspect that even with my meager supply of faith I
am standing in grace. I need only open my eyes to
see the hem of God's garment waiting for my touch.

I touch the hem of Jesus' garment each time I celebrate the Eucharist or participate in the sacraments. Every leaf, every blade of grass—indeed the entire created universe—are all parts of the holy tassel of the Divine. Every considerate act is a touching of the hem. There are times when I too risk my reputation as I push through the crowds, daring to take my stand for what I believe in. All praise to that daring, faith-filled woman who could be you or me!

O lifelong Teacher,

Help me walk through this week aware of my need for healing. The earth has been blessed with your overwhelming presence. Open my eyes to see that the tassel of your robe, the hem of your garment, is everywhere. Take away my fear of walking through the crowds, claiming my belief in you. Reveal to me that I am standing knee-deep in grace, with the tassel of your cloak in reach. Amen.

Your teacher for this week is *the hem of God's garment*. Look for it everywhere, and reach for it when you are in need of healing.

> We, too, can experience power
> flowing out of us and into us
> if we but open our eyes.
> A gentle embrace is a power exchange.
> Opening an orange for someone with arthritic fingers
> is touching the hem of the garment.
> Beholding a flower is touching the hem.
> The whole world is God's garment.
> If we learn to live awake
> we will experience Christ-Power
> flowing out to us, then from us to others.
>   —Macrina Wiederkehr

WEEK **THIRTY-EIGHT**

Read 2 Timothy 4:9–17, attempting to feel as Paul must have felt.

> Try to join me soon, for Demas, enamored of the present world, deserted me and went to Thessalonica, Crescens to Galatia, and Titus to Dalmatia. Luke is the only one with me. Get Mark and bring him with you, for he is helpful to me in the ministry. I have sent Tychicus to Ephesus. When you come, bring the cloak I left with Carpus in Troas, the papyrus rolls, and especially the parchments.
>
> Alexander the coppersmith did me a great deal of harm; the Lord will repay him according to his deeds. You too be on guard against him, for he has strongly resisted our preaching.

> At my first defense no one appeared on my behalf, but everyone deserted me. May it not be held against them! But the Lord stood by me and gave me strength, so that through me the proclamation might be completed and all the Gentiles might hear it. And I was rescued from the lion's mouth.

A shadow of loneliness encompasses this passage from 2 Timothy. Paul is feeling deserted, abandoned, and alone. He has encountered resistance to the message of Jesus that he has been proclaiming. There is even a hint of betrayal. He is having a taste of the discouragement that every minister of the Word of God experiences from time to time.

Perhaps this is not so unusual. If everyone likes what you're saying, you had better check to see if it is really the Word of God you are preaching. Jesus left no doubt about the struggles that those who speak for God would eventually encounter.

Paul is a beautiful teacher for all of us discouraged ministers of the Word. In between the mixture of feelings with which he is struggling, we see also the welcoming face of forgiveness. Following the example of Jesus, he asks that nothing be held against his offenders. He is also a role model for us in that he asks for help. With his plea, "Get Mark," he is admitting that he can't carry on alone. He needs the support of other faithful believers.

Jesus,

When we are weighed down with discouragement, show us your face. Spend time with us. Take away the veil that prevents us from sensing your presence. Support us and restore our lost courage. Send help!

Your teacher for this week is *someone who is lonely, someone who needs you.* Look around you with insightful eyes. Each day choose someone you can reach out to and learn from.

Compassion asks us to go where it hurts, to enter into the places of pain,
to share in brokenness, fear, confusion, and anguish.

Compassion challenges us to cry out with those
in misery,
to mourn with those who are lonely, to weep with
those in tears.
Compassion requires us to be weak with the weak,
vulnerable with the vulnerable,
and powerless with the powerless.
Compassion means full immersion
in the condition of being human.

–Henri Nouwen

WEEK **THIRTY-NINE**

Prayerfully read John 21:15–19. How does your love need to be renewed?

> When they had finished breakfast, Jesus said to Simon Peter, "Simon, son of John, do you love me more than these?" He said to him, "Yes, Lord, you know that I love you." He said to him, "Feed my lambs." He then said to him a second time, "Simon, son of John, do you love me?" He said to him, "Yes, Lord, you know that I love you." He said to him, "Tend my sheep." He said to him the third time, "Simon, son of John, do you love me?" Peter was distressed that he had said to him a third time, "Do you love me?" and he said to him, "Lord, you know everything; you know that I love you." [Jesus] said to him, "Feed my

sheep. Amen, amen, I say to you, when you were younger, you used to dress yourself and go where you wanted; but when you grow old, you will stretch out your hands, and someone else will dress you and lead you where you do not want to go." He said this signifying by what kind of death he would glorify God. And when he had said this, he said to him, "Follow me."

Dear humbled Peter, when questioned about his precarious love, gives an unwavering answer: "Yes, Lord, you know that I love you." There is little doubt in my mind that Peter experienced some anguish in hearing Jesus' question. Three times he was tormented with that question: "Peter, do you love me?" I have often wondered about this poignant encounter between Peter and Jesus. After their breakfast on the beach, did Jesus pull Peter aside so this vulnerable issue could be discussed in private? Or were the other apostles in earshot of the questioning?

It was fear that crowded out Peter's love at the time of his denial. Now he is given the opportunity to replace his fear with an affirmation of love. In 1 John 4:18 it is explained that perfect love casts out fear. We can turn that sentence around and declare that perfect fear casts out love also.

Perhaps that is what happened to Peter at the time of his denial: his perfect fear smothered his love. Now in the wake of Jesus' resurrection, his love seems stronger than his fear. Have you, like Peter, had the experience of juggling fear and love in your life?

Lord of the Resurrection,

Today I echo Peter's acclamation of love. Yes, Lord, I love you! I love you as well as I know how in the midst of all my fears and my reluctance to be your disciple. Deepen my love. Smother my fears. Teacher, show me the way to your heart. Convince me that there are no shortcuts. I must walk through all my hesitancy and excuses. I must wade through my fears and my lack of trust until I see your face, O God. I have been praying for a glimpse of that face of love for a long time, Lord. Give me the courage to desire that my prayers

*be answered. Give me faith to believe in those
answered prayers. Amen and amen.*

Your teacher for the week is *Peter's proclamation of
love.* What can it teach you about humility, fear,
grace, and forgiveness?

There is no fear in love, . . .
perfect love casts out fear.

–1 John 4:18 (NRSV)

WEEK **FORTY**

Read 2 Corinthians 3:1–6. Consider the ways you are a letter from Christ.

> Are we beginning to commend ourselves again? Or do we need, as some do, letters of recommendation to you or from you? You are our letter, written on our hearts, known and read by all, and shown to be a letter of Christ administered by us, written not in ink but by the Spirit of the living God, not on tablets of stone but on tablets that are hearts of flesh.
>
> Such confidence we have through Christ toward God. Not that of ourselves we are qualified to take credit for anything as coming from us; rather, our qualification comes from God, who has indeed qualified us as ministers of a new

covenant, not of letter but of spirit; for the
letter brings death, but the Spirit gives life.

"Not that of ourselves we are qualified to take credit
for anything as coming from us; rather, our qual-
ification comes from God." There are times when
these words annoy me. I'd like to think I have a few
qualifications of my own. However, when I take
these words to prayer, my attitude changes drastical-
ly. I am filled with joy in remembering that, because
I belong to God, there is a sacredness in my life that
equips me for ministry. I receive my qualifications
from the spirit within me. All is gift.

We are ministers of a new covenant where the
emphasis is placed on spirit rather than law. The law
is given to help us find the spirit that is already in us;
it is not an end in and of itself. People may mouth
the law to impress others or to lord it over them,
yet if our focus is on the spirit, our teaching will
show itself as love rather than law even as we follow
the law's commandments. This is what happened in
the life of Jesus. Indeed, this may be the reason he
was killed. He seemed, at times, disrespectful of the

law. Perhaps this is because he was in touch with an unseeable inner law.

What happened to Jesus happens to us. God's glory marries our own little spark of light, and a new radiance is displayed in our lives. We become a letter of Christ written by the spirit of the living God. It is God's love in us that qualifies us to be ministers for Christ.

Spirit of the living God,

Write your law within my heart. It is your love within me that equips me to be your minister. It is your Spirit within that fills me with abundant life. Awaken me to this gift. It is easy to sleepwalk through life, pretending that if I keep all the rules and laws, I am special. Uncover the truth and reveal to me that I am special because your Spirit abides in me. Then all those laws that seemed so difficult at first will become a joy to my heart. May it be so!

Your teacher for this week will be *your gifts for ministry*. Not with pride but in all humility claim the gifts

God has given you and allow them to teach you. Each day this week, name one of your gifts, cherish it, and use it. This may be scary. It is difficult for most of us to own the gifts God has given us. But for God's sake, let us try.

> There is an experience of the Eternal
> breaking into time, which transforms all life
> into a miracle of faith and action.
>
> –Thomas Kelly

WEEK **FORTY-ONE**

Read Luke 9:7–9. Like Herod, yet hopefully for the right reasons, keep trying to see Jesus.

> Herod the tetrarch heard about all that was happening, and he was greatly perplexed because some were saying, "John has been raised from the dead"; others were saying, "Elijah has appeared"; still others, "One of the ancient prophets has arisen." But Herod said, "John I beheaded. Who then is this about whom I hear such things?" And he kept trying to see him.

Curiosity is not a sin; in fact, it may be one of our forgotten virtues. To be curious about something or someone can open up new avenues of learning, awareness, and knowledge. Curiosity can be the beginning of an emerging creativity. It can even be the beginning of a deep faith.

Thus, Herod's curiosity about Jesus had the potential of blossoming into understanding, perhaps even into friendship. Unfortunately, his curiosity did not lead him to these growing places or to faith. It led instead to resentment and jealousy. Above all, it led to fear and thus became his downfall.

What about us? Do we have purposeful curiosity? Does our curiosity open us to new possibilities? Are we able to see the healthy aspect of curiosity, or are we stuck with old attitudes that can only see curiosity as prying into what is none of our business?

If you're full of love, the things you pry into will always be for the good of others.

Creative One,

Fill my heart with questions; make of me a pondering soul, inquisitive, open to exploration, and full of wonder. Open my mind to mysteries. I want to know all that you have in store for me. Give me a Christlike heart that never stops

opening. O Holy One, gift me with good curiosity.
Help me to keep on trying to see Jesus. Amen.

You've guessed it! Your teacher for this week is *curiosity*. Where might it lead you? What can it teach you?

> Somewhere,
> something incredible
> is waiting to be known.
>
>   –Blaise Pascal

WEEK **FORTY-TWO**

Read Romans 8:26–27, and ponder your own inability to pray as you ought.

> In the same way, the Spirit too comes to the aid of our weakness; for we do not know how to pray as we ought, but the Spirit itself intercedes with inexpressible groanings. And the one who searches hearts knows what is the intention of the Spirit, because it intercedes for the holy ones according to God's will.

These are words I can taste. There are times when I suspect the Spirit is praying in me and I just need to shut up and listen. When deciding what words to use for prayer, I am often at a loss. My poor words limp when I attempt to share the deepest yearnings of my soul. What a grace it would be if I could learn to trust those wordless groanings deep in the recesses of my soul as the Spirit actually praying in me! Do I believe that the One who searches my heart understands the wordless language of the Spirit? Can I find enough trust to let go of trying to find just the right words when I pray? Do I believe that the Spirit is able to recognize my needs and intercede to God for me? Can I believe that the emptiness I sometimes feel is, in reality, the grace of God opening and emptying me so that the Spirit can blow through the fragile reed of my life?

Those of us who love words would do well to continue pondering the meaning of this text. I believe that many of us experience groanings in the depths of our being, groanings that are too deep for words. As we become attentive to the Spirit's pervading presence in our lives, it is probable that each of us will shelter yearnings that cannot be expressed in speech. Through God's grace, we will begin to trust that this mysterious inner presence is the guardian of our yearnings. Then perhaps we can rest in the meadow of no words and let God's marvelous work begin.

Spirit of the living God,
     Read my heart! Read it quietly for your own understanding of me. Then read it to me slowly that I might understand the language of your inexpressible groaning within me. O you who know well my unspoken yearnings, teach me to trust your silent presence and your wordless love. May it come to pass!

Your teacher for the week is *the groaning of the Spirit within*. To get in touch with this teacher you will need to become very quiet, empty, and open. What can you learn from the Spirit's groanings and your yearnings? Are they one and the same?

All life has emptiness at its core.
It is the quiet hollow reed through which
the wind of God blows
and makes the music that is our life.
                                        –Wayne Muller

WEEK **FORTY-THREE**

As you read Matthew 13:31–35 ponder this truth: from the small gifts in your life, God has done wonders.

> [Jesus] proposed another parable to them. "The kingdom of heaven is like a mustard seed that a person took and sowed in a field. It is the smallest of all the seeds, yet when full-grown it is the largest of plants. It becomes a large bush, and the 'birds of the sky come and dwell in its branches.'"
>
> He spoke to them another parable. "The kingdom of heaven is like yeast that a woman took and mixed with three measures of wheat flour until the whole batch was leavened."
>
> All these things Jesus spoke to the crowds in parables. He spoke to them only

in parables, to fulfill what had been said
through the prophet:

"I will open my mouth in parables,
     I will announce what has lain hid-
          den from the foundation [of
          the world]."

Tiny things, and especially seeds, have often been a
source of inspiration for me. When I am attentive
to the hidden possibility of a seed, reverence wells
up in me. I am in awe. What a mystery it is with its
potential to break open and pour out new life! How
amazing to watch the growth of tiny things!

In our gospel reflection for this week, the emphasis is placed on the smallness of the seed. How can
something so small become so magnificent? Imagine for a moment how small you were on the day
of your birth. You, too, grew from a seed. Like the
mustard seed, you are filled with budding possibilities for growth.

Rejoice in the truth that God once breathed
upon the tiny seed of you. God honored your smallness, and you blossomed into a remarkable tree of
life. You, too, are a sign of the reign of God. The

leaven of your little life lived with faithfulness can support those who are struggling to grow stronger in their relationship with God. This week practice believing in the potential of small things. Even a tiny desire to forgive someone is full of possibility. That small desire is a seed that needs to be nurtured and believed in so that it can blossom.

O Creator and Lover of small things,

Thank you for all the little things that flourish and grow to summits of immense beauty. All of creation is permeated with your sacred power. Teach me to be grateful for the many little things whose vocations are just to be small. Small is beautiful and contains the power it needs to do its work. Small hopes, small dreams, and small efforts are not insignificant. In the miniscule and in the vast your power shines forth. May you be praised in all things!

Your teacher for this week will be *the small things* in your life. During this week, find a few small things and learn from them.

He showed me a little thing, the size of a hazel nut. . . .
In this little thing I saw three properties.
The first is that God made it.
The second that God loves it.
And the third, that God keeps it.

—Julian of Norwich

WEEK **FORTY-FOUR**

As you read Luke 12:1–7, try to lovingly embrace all within you that you would like to hide. In that embrace you will find freedom.

> Meanwhile, so many people were crowding together that they were trampling one another underfoot. [Jesus] began to speak, first to his disciples, "Beware of the leaven—that is, the hypocrisy—of the Pharisees.
>
> "There is nothing concealed that will not be revealed, nor secret that will not be known. Therefore whatever you have said in the darkness will be heard in the light, and what you have whispered behind closed doors will be proclaimed on the housetops. I tell you, my friends, do not be afraid of those who kill the body but after that can do no more. I shall show

> you whom to fear. Be afraid of the one
> who after killing has the power to cast
> into Gehenna; yes, I tell you, be afraid of
> that one. Are not five sparrows sold for
> two small coins? Yet not one of them has
> escaped the notice of God. Even the hairs
> of your head have all been counted. Do
> not be afraid. You are worth more than
> many sparrows."

To be told that all our actions, words, and thoughts
will be made known can be a bit unnerving. Most
of us don't aspire to be known quite so thoroughly.
However, if we look perceptively into our hearts,
we may be surprised to discover a secret desire *to be
known*. To be known and loved with all of our weaknesses and limitations can be immensely freeing. It
can also be terrifying.

Jesus asks us today to guard against the yeast of
the Pharisees that, he says, is hypocrisy. Perhaps by
using the word *yeast* Jesus is suggesting that, just as
yeast grows, all within us that is false can easily grow
if we do not keep a check on it. Let us keep loving
guard over our souls. Our bodies can be destroyed,
but the soul belongs entirely to God.

We are better, Jesus says, than a whole flock of sparrows. That may not sound like much of a compliment, but in some perplexing way Jesus is telling us that we are precious. We are known by heart. Even the hairs of our head are counted. Does the idea of being utterly known by God frighten or console you? The answer to this question may depend on what kind of yeast you are nurturing.

Jesus, life of my soul,
Help me to look at being known as a gift to celebrate rather than as an enslaving yoke to fear. May your knowing me set me free!

Let your teacher for this week be the truth of *being known by God*. Simply sit and walk with this truth for a little while each day this week. What can being known teach you?

The lamplight of God's eye shines
upon our sins and weaknesses,
our sorrows and despair, our fears, our joys,

our anger, our dreams, our love, our heart's yearnings.
All is known. Nothing is hidden.
A change sometimes occurs in our lives
when we are able to accept God's knowing gaze.
Slowly the "knowing of God"
begins to console us rather than frighten us.

—Macrina Wiederkehr

WEEK **FORTY-FIVE**

Read Matthew 13:44–52. Could the kingdom of heaven be hidden in you?

> [Jesus said,] "The kingdom of heaven is like a treasure buried in a field, which a person finds and hides again, and out of joy goes and sells all that he has and buys that field. Again, the kingdom of heaven is like a merchant searching for fine pearls. When he finds a pearl of great price, he goes and sells all that he has and buys it. Again, the kingdom of heaven is like a net thrown into the sea, which collects fish of every kind. When it is full they haul it ashore and sit down to put what is good into buckets. What is bad they throw away. Thus it will be at the end of the age. The angels will go out and separate the wicked from the

righteous and throw them into the fiery furnace, where there will be wailing and grinding of teeth.

"Do you understand all these things?" They answered, "Yes." And he replied, "Then every scribe who has been instructed in the kingdom of heaven is like the head of a household who brings from his storeroom both the new and the old."

These little parables make it clear that the kingdom of heaven is not just handed to you. It is not always visible, although it is in our midst. To find that space where God lives, one must search, discover, and make choices. Sometimes we may even need to ask the way to the treasure. We need teachers and guides. Alexandra Trenfor offers us much wisdom in these lovely words, "The best teachers are those who show you where to look, but don't tell you what to see."

The people who found the hidden treasure and the pearl in our gospel reflection for this week did not totally claim the treasure upon first finding it. The treasure had to be earned. Possessions and agendas had to be relinquished. Surrender had to take place in the heart so that the discoverer of the treasure could recognize that the reign of God begins right there in the emptied heart. Try to identify with the one who found the treasure. What would you need to dispose of in order to give yourself entirely to the treasure?

Use your imagination as you symbolically throw a net into the sea of your heart. What is buried in your own life? You may be surprised at what you haul in. There will be riches and treasures; there will be debris and rubbish that act as hindrances and obstacles. Evaluate what you need to live a holy, purposeful life. How can you live on the earth and be faithful to the reign of God *already in your midst*? What does selling all you have to obtain the pearl of great price mean to you?

These are not questions that can be easily answered. Rather, they are mysteries to prayerfully ponder. There are treasures in our lives that are not visible at first glance. To enjoy these treasures will require space for concentrated and prayerful solitude. This will also entail a sacred loneliness well known to those who search for God. You are already on that quest. May the reign of God choose you!

O hidden God of the parables,
*   May your stories come true in my life! Give me a heart hungry enough to surrender everything for the treasure so that you will always be the source of my life. Give me enough loneliness that I will never turn away from the quest. O let it be!*

Your teacher for the week is *the sacred loneliness* that companions you in your search for the Divine. Allow yourself to experience the loneliness. Make friends with it. Dialogue with it. It will teach you how to keep your ache alive on your journey to the treasure.

Pray that your loneliness may spur you into finding something to live for, great enough to die for.
                                        –Dag Hammarskjöld

WEEK **FORTY-SIX**

Read 2 Corinthians 5:14–21 with your heart set on being an ambassador for Christ.

> For the love of Christ impels us, once we have come to the conviction that one died for all; therefore, all have died. He indeed died for all, so that those who live might no longer live for themselves but for him who for their sake died and was raised.
>
> Consequently, from now on we regard no one according to the flesh; even if we once knew Christ according to the flesh, yet now we know him so no longer. So whoever is in Christ is a new creation: the old things have passed away; behold, new things have come. And all this is from God, who has reconciled us to himself through Christ and given us the ministry

of reconciliation, namely, God was reconciling the world to himself in Christ, not counting their trespasses against them and entrusting to us the message of reconciliation. So we are ambassadors for Christ, as if God were appealing through us. We implore you on behalf of Christ, be reconciled to God. For our sake he made him to be sin who did not know sin, so that we might become the righteousness of God in him.

Very simply said: We represent Christ in the world. We embody Christ. We speak for him. We are a vessel of Christ-life. All the works we undertake, the words we speak, the art we create, and the melodies we compose have the potential of reproducing Christ's image in our world. Nowhere is this described more beautifully than in a prayer attributed to St. Teresa of Avila, suggesting that Christ has no body on earth today except ours. Ours are the eyes through which his compassion gazes upon the world. Ours are the feet with which he walks through the world ministering to others.

Throughout this week, practice remembering that you are an ambassador for Christ. You speak to those who do not understand his language. Are your actions reminiscent of the life he led? Do your words exemplify his spirit? What does seeing with the eyes of Christ mean to you? Does the love of Christ impel you to live no longer for yourself but for the One who died for you? Does the love of Christ summon you to live for others? How has the work of reconciliation become a ministry in your life? How have you been reconciled to God?

O Christ of faith,

Make of me a new creation. Work miracles through me. Do not allow me to be separated from you or from others. Give me the vision to unify what is divided. Teach me the art of being a reconciler in our world. May the ministry of reconciling the world to God become a rising sun in my life. O let it be!

The work of reconciliation never ceases. Your teacher for this week is *the reconciliation* that must yet take place in your life. Each day of this week, choose one area in your life where understanding is needed. It can be within you, with someone else, or with God. Reconciliation is the best way to become a new person. What can you learn from that which is not yet resolved in your life?

We are called to be "ambassadors for Christ."
Ours is a ministry of reconciliation. . . .
To be an ambassador for Christ means
above all to invite everyone
to a renewed personal relationship
with the Lord Jesus.

–Pope Francis

WEEK **FORTY-SEVEN**

As you read Genesis 1:1–29, make a conscious effort to visualize the story. Read slowly, pausing to literally see the birthing of creation.

> In the beginning, when God created the heavens and the earth—and the earth was without form or shape, with darkness over the abyss and a mighty wind sweeping over the waters—
>
> Then God said: Let there be light, and there was light. God saw that the light was good. God then separated the light from the darkness. God called the light "day," and the darkness he called "night." Evening came, and morning followed—the first day.
>
> Then God said: Let there be a dome in the middle of the waters, to separate one body of water from the other. God

made the dome, and it separated the water below the dome from the water above the dome. And so it happened. God called the dome "sky." Evening came, and morning followed—the second day.

Then God said: Let the water under the sky be gathered into a single basin, so that the dry land may appear. And so it happened: the water under the sky was gathered into its basin, and the dry land appeared. God called the dry land "earth," and the basin of water he called "sea." God saw that it was good. Then God said: Let the earth bring forth vegetation: every kind of plant that bears seed and every kind of fruit tree on earth that bears fruit with its seed in it. And so it happened: the earth brought forth vegetation: every kind of plant that bears seed and every kind of fruit tree that bears fruit with its seed in it. God saw that it was good. Evening came, and morning followed—the third day.

Then God said: Let there be lights in the dome of the sky, to separate day from night. Let them mark the seasons, the days and the years, and serve as lights in the dome of the sky, to illuminate the earth. And so it happened: God made the two great lights, the greater one to govern the day, and the lesser one to govern the night, and the stars. God set them in the dome of the sky, to illuminate the earth, to govern the day and the night, and to separate the light from the darkness. God saw that it was good. Evening came, and morning followed—the fourth day.

Then God said: Let the water teem with an abundance of living creatures, and on the earth let birds fly beneath the dome of the sky. God created the great sea monsters and all kinds of crawling living creatures with which the water teems, and all kinds of winged birds. God saw that it was good, and God blessed them, saying: Be fertile, multiply, and fill the water of the seas; and let the birds multiply on the earth. Evening came, and morning followed—the fifth day.

Then God said: Let the earth bring forth every kind of living creature: tame animals, crawling things, and every kind of wild animal. And so it happened: God made every kind of wild animal, every kind of tame animal, and every kind of thing that crawls on the ground. God saw that it was good. Then God said: Let us make human beings in our image, after our likeness. Let them have dominion over the fish of the sea, the birds of the air, the tame animals, all the wild animals, and all the creatures that crawl on the earth.

God created mankind in his image;
in the image of God he created
them;
male and female he created them.

God blessed them and God said to them: Be fertile and multiply; fill the earth and subdue it. Have dominion over the fish of the sea, the birds of the air, and all the living things that crawl on the earth. God also said: See, I give you every seed-bearing plant on all the earth and every tree that has seed-bearing fruit on it to be your food.

A story can be a wondrous container for a truth that must be told. The Genesis story tells of the love of a creative God lifting beauty and order out of chaos. This delightful creation story depicts the artistic unfolding of the universe. It highlights the goodness of all that is being created. It also reminds us of our fundamental responsibility to care for the earth.

As you read the story, invite your senses to companion you in the reading. See it all happening. Be still and listen to the mighty wind sweeping over the dark waters. Imagine the wind being the breath of God, the spirit of God. We have seen how wind blows things out of old places into new places. That which is intended to be gift for us is being blown into its rightful place. Slowly the light and the darkness emerge. The waters separate; the sky becomes visible. The rhythm of day and night, morning and evening, is revealed. The dry lands and the seas appear. And oh, that marvelous moment when things begin to grow! Smell the earthiness of it all. The earth makes known its potential to produce fruits, vegetables, and all kinds of plants—all because of the sun and the moon, the balance of light and darkness.

God then created us. We are sometimes called the crown of creation, yet how easy it is to forget our responsibility to care for the earth as it cares for us! We who have been created in God's image so often forget that we bear the divine imprint. Does the mighty wind that once swept over the waters of chaos need to sweep over our troubled lives again?

Loving Creator,

How easy it is to forget that we are created in your image. In the portrayal of your creative work you have told the story of the goodness of the earth. Give us the heart of a gardener that we may lovingly tend the work you have begun. Raise up grateful friends of the earth to sustain her. Help us to be ever mindful of the divine imprint in our souls. O you who holds the earth in the palm of your hands, hear us and hold us. Amen.

Let *the earth* be your teacher. Spend some time outside each day this week.

We depend on nature not only for our
physical survival.
We also need nature to show us the way home
out of the prison of our own minds. . . .
We have forgotten what rocks, plants,
and animals still know.
We have forgotten how to be . . .
to be where the life is:
Here and Now.

                                        –Eckhart Tolle

WEEK **FORTY-EIGHT**

Read Mark 12:28–34. Meditate on what an immense compliment it is to us that God believes we can love with such totality.

> One of the scribes, when he came forward and heard them disputing and saw how well he had answered them, asked him, "Which is the first of all the commandments?" Jesus replied, "The first is this: 'Hear, O Israel! The Lord our God is Lord alone! You shall love the Lord your God with all your heart, with all your soul, with all your mind, and with all your strength.' The second is this: 'You shall love your neighbor as yourself.' There is no other commandment greater than these." The scribe said to him, "Well said, teacher. You are right in saying, 'He is One and there is no

other than he.' And 'to love him with all your heart, with all your understanding, with all your strength, and to love your neighbor as yourself' is worth more than all burnt offerings and sacrifices." And when Jesus saw that [he] answered with understanding, he said to him, "You are not far from the kingdom of God." And no one dared to ask him any more questions.

Heart! Soul! Mind! Strength! We are to love God with our entire beings. All of it! I am to love others and myself in this same way. In this well-known scripture text from the Gospel of Mark, Jesus has chosen to reiterate what, in my deepest heart, I already know. I am made for love. And yet, can I claim to know what I do not fully live? Who can love like this? It's the word *all* that is frightening. Rumi, one of the mystic poets of the East, suggests that in order to bring a whole heart home to God, we have to dismiss our half loves. Wonderful as that idea may sound, I, who have so many half loves, find it both demanding and attractive. It's a struggle to be obedient to the demand that I love with all my heart.

In one of her children's books, *A Wind in the Door*, Madeleine L'Engle writes of a cherubim who has come from another planet to teach Meg to love unconditionally. The cherubim says, "You're full of love, Meg, but you don't know how to stay with it in the hard times." We probably all struggle to stay with love in the hard times. Love is to be lived even in the hard times. Love is a treasure. It is the diamond for which we are searching. A diamond comes from heat and pressure formed deep in the earth's heart.

When it comes to love, we are not always diamonds. Purification awaits us. We are, however, to love others and ourselves even in the evolving process. Let there be love!

O God of love,

Must everything be in order before you recognize my love? Aren't you satisfied with my partly open, partly ready heart? Isn't it better than a closed heart? As I move into this week with my

*half love and my half heart, I trust I am on my way
to learning how to love with a fully open heart.
I trust also that you love me in all my stages of
growth. O you who are still watching me take
shape, save me from my fear of purification. Let
my life continue to unfold. Yes.*

Your *half love* is to be your teacher this week. What
can you learn from it?

> Love is patient; love is kind;
> Love is not envious, or boastful
> or arrogant or rude.
> It does not insist on its own way;
> It is not irritable or resentful.
>
> —1 Corinthians 13:4–5 (NRSV)

WEEK **FORTY-NINE**

As you read Luke 6:37–42, ask for the grace to truly know yourself.

> [Jesus said,] "Stop judging and you will not be judged. Stop condemning and you will not be condemned. Forgive and you will be forgiven. Give and gifts will be given to you; a good measure, packed together, shaken down, and overflowing, will be poured into your lap. For the measure with which you measure will in return be measured out to you." And he told them a parable, "Can a blind person guide a blind person? Will not both fall into a pit? No disciple is superior to the teacher; but when fully trained, every disciple will be like his teacher. Why do you notice the splinter in your brother's eye, but do not perceive the wooden

> beam in your own? How can you say
> to your brother, 'Brother, let me remove
> that splinter in your eye,' when you do
> not even notice the wooden beam in
> your own eye? You hypocrite! Remove
> the wooden beam from your eye first;
> then you will see clearly to remove the
> splinter in your brother's eye."

To know ourselves with all of our flaws, weaknesses,
and sins is a precious gift. It may not seem so precious, at first, as we come face-to-face with things
in our lives that we would like to hide. Often what
we dislike in another person is a reflection of some
hidden enemy in our own life. The other person
becomes a mirror for us. We see in this person what
we don't like in ourselves. If we practice being grateful for such persons in our lives, they can become
our teachers. Today, then, while meditating on
beams, planks, and splinters, let's take a long, hon-
est, yet gentle look at ourselves. What we see will
not kill us; it may give us new life.

Sometimes our sins become our blessings. They
can pierce our hearts and unveil our vulnerabilities.

They can open our eyes to the truth that we all need forgiveness. Learning to reflect on our frailties and flaws can draw from us compassion for the weaknesses of others. So let's pray for the gift of self-understanding. Perhaps we will become more aware of the reality that we walk together here on earth and share each other's splinters.

O deep-seeing One,
*   May the weaknesses and sins I see in others become a school of self-knowledge for me. Teach me tenderness for the frailty of others, for they are mirrors reflecting my own face. Clothe me with garments of compassion and encouragement, that I may learn to love as you love. May my prayer come true!*

An interesting teacher this week: *the sins and weaknesses of others*. Find your own face in their weaknesses. Pray for them. Pray for insight for yourself.

We are all capable
of one another's faults.

                              –Jane Frances de Chantal

WEEK **FIFTY**

Read Luke 6:12–19, asking for insight to recognize the areas where you need healing.

> In those days [Jesus] departed to the mountain to pray, and he spent the night in prayer to God. When day came, he called his disciples to himself, and from them he chose Twelve, whom he also named apostles: Simon, whom he named Peter, and his brother Andrew, James, John, Philip, Bartholomew, Matthew, Thomas, James the son of Alphaeus, Simon who was called a Zealot, and Judas the son of James, and Judas Iscariot, who became a traitor.
>
> And he came down with them and stood on a stretch of level ground. A great crowd of his disciples and a large number of the people from all Judea and Jerusalem

> and the coastal region of Tyre and Sidon
> came to hear him and to be healed of
> their diseases; and even those who were
> tormented by unclean spirits were cured.
> Everyone in the crowd sought to touch
> him because power came forth from him
> and healed them all.

Where did Jesus get this power? How did he become a healer? How did he replenish his own spirit when people needing healing, encouragement, and comfort drained away his power? It's too easy to dismiss these questions with a quick answer such as, *Jesus was God. He had an infinite source of divine strength.* Jesus was also human with a body that felt the same weariness we feel. There were times when, like us, he felt abandoned and discouraged. He must have known the agony of wondering where he was going to glean the energy for his next work of love.

This scripture text from Luke makes a strong statement about Jesus' wisdom in learning how to care for his soul. Jesus spent the night in communion with God. After that long night of prayer, he chose the apostles who were to companion him in his ministry.

There are other episodes in the scriptures that depict Jesus spending long hours in prayer before or after significant moments in his ministry. In doing this, Jesus models for us how we are to replenish our power supply. We cannot continue working at fever pitch. We must find ways to renew our spirits. How can you restore the physical and spiritual energy in your life?

Restorer of energy,

Lead me back to the source of my strength and power—the source that is you. Convince me that I have time to go away to pray, to listen, and to restore my spirit. Assure me that I do not have to be flawless to be your instrument of healing. Give me the kind of trust that enables me to believe that because I belong to you I, too, have a healing power that comes from heaven. O let it be true!

Your teacher for this week is *your own power to be a healer*. You will need to be intentionally present throughout the hours of this week. This mindfulness will lead you to the source of your power.

Nobody escapes being wounded.
We are all wounded people, whether
physically, emotionally, mentally, or spiritually.
The main question is not
"How can we hide our wounds?"
so we don't have to be embarrassed, but
"How can we put our woundedness
in the service of others?"
When our wounds cease to be a source of shame,
and become a source of healing,
we have become wounded healers.

–Henri Nouwen

WEEK **FIFTY-ONE**

In reading James 5:13–20, ask yourself if there is any obstacle to grace (sin), deterring you from being your best self. If so, to whom might you confess this?

> Is anyone among you suffering? He should pray. Is anyone in good spirits? He should sing praise. Is anyone among you sick? He should summon the presbyters of the church, and they should pray over him and anoint [him] with oil in the name of the Lord, and the prayer of faith will save the sick person, and the Lord will raise him up. If he has committed any sins, he will be forgiven.
>
> Therefore, confess your sins to one another and pray for one another, that you may be healed. The fervent prayer of a righteous person is very powerful. Elijah

was a human being like us; yet he prayed
earnestly that it might not rain, and for
three years and six months it did not rain
upon the land. Then he prayed again, and
the sky gave rain and the earth produced
its fruit.

My brothers [and sisters], if anyone
among you should stray from the truth
and someone bring him back, he should
know that whoever brings back a sinner
from the error of his way will save his soul
from death and will cover a multitude of
sins.

We are asked to pray when we are suffering, to sing
when we are in good spirits. If our loved ones are
sick, we are to call in faith-filled people. Our joy and
sorrow, our sickness and health, can be living prayers
if we enter into these experiences intentionally.

Whether we are suffering or in good spirits,
let us turn to the One who companions both our
broken and joyful hearts. There are times when we
underestimate the power of prayer. We can go to
prayer rather casually, not expecting much to take

place. It's a good habit to be there, but we haven't brought our hearts along.

Even when it appears that nothing is happening—when God has taken a cruise for all we know—what is actually unfolding may catch up with us later. We ought never to judge our prayer by how we feel. When we pray with a community of believers, someone else's faith may supply what is lacking in ours. This is the time to believe that every prayer has its own guardian angel. Sometimes the angel of prayer cradles us with tenderness and anoints us with the oil of patience and hope. At other times the angel of prayer skips along beside us, lifting our spirits higher, that we may discover an even deeper joy. And of course there are times when the angel of prayer kneels before us as with Jesus in the Garden of Gethsemane. The angel of prayer observes our moods and tries to honor them.

O Angel of prayer,

Inspire me to pray always. Guide me through all of life that I may experience the divine presence in sickness and in health, in times of suffering and in times of happiness, and in my dying and in my living. O wise Teacher, help me to believe that there is no such thing as a lost prayer. Make of my life a living prayer.

Let the *power of prayer* be your teacher. Each time you sit down to pray this week, try to sense a sacred presence surrounding you. Pay attention to this presence, and your day just might unfold in unexpected ways.

> Prayer is nothing but oneness with Christ.
> As scripture says in St. Paul,
> "I live no longer, but Christ lives in me."
> Christ prays in me,
> Christ thinks in me,
> Christ looks through my eyes,
> Christ speaks through my words,
> Christ works with my hands,
> Christ walks with my feet,
> Christ loves with my heart.
>
> —St. Teresa of Calcutta

WEEK **FIFTY-TWO**

As you read Luke 2:22–35, consider the moments when you have waited for Christ.

> When the days were completed for their purification according to the law of Moses, [Mary and Joseph] took [Jesus] up to Jerusalem to present him to the Lord, just as it is written in the law of the Lord, "Every male that opens the womb shall be consecrated to the Lord," and to offer the sacrifice of "a pair of turtledoves or two young pigeons," in accordance with the dictate in the law of the Lord.
>
> Now there was a man in Jerusalem whose name was Simeon. This man was righteous and devout, awaiting the consolation of Israel, and the holy Spirit was upon him. It had been revealed to him by the holy Spirit that he should not see

death before he had seen the Messiah of
the Lord. He came in the Spirit into the
temple; and when the parents brought in
the child Jesus to perform the custom of
the law in regard to him, he took him into
his arms and blessed God, saying:

> "Now, Master, you may let your ser-
>   vant go
>   in peace, according to your word,
> for my eyes have seen your salvation,
>   which you prepared in sight of all
>   the peoples,
> a light for revelation to the Gentiles,
>   and glory for your people Israel."

The child's father and mother were
amazed at what was said about him;
and Simeon blessed them and said to
Mary his mother, "Behold, this child
is destined for the fall and rise of many
in Israel, and to be a sign that will be
contradicted (and you yourself a sword
will pierce) so that the thoughts of many
hearts may be revealed."

Simeon's words offer us a prayer of serenity and fulfillment. His life is coming to an end. Now that his eyes have beheld the glory of Jesus, the anointed one, he is ready to hand over his soul to the infinite mystery that comes with death. This is his swan song.

Over the years this canticle has been chanted in the night office of the Church. These words serve as a perfect prayer for the closing day. At the end of each day, we proclaim that we have seen the light of revelation: the face of God. That which is sacred is hidden in full view. It is our open eyes and attentive hearts that enable us to witness the wonders of God's presence at every moment.

Our night prayer is our swan song. We are retiring. The day is complete. We offer a grateful prayer for the day's blessings and ask protection for the night. We do not know if we will awake in the morning. In the Rule of St. Benedict, we are asked to keep death daily before our eyes. It is the other side of life. It reminds us that we are frail and glorious human beings.

At the night hour, with Simeon, we are grateful for what our eyes have seen. Christ has been revealed to us this day in countless ways. Tonight before retiring, kneel by your bedside in the darkness or stand at your window looking out into the night. Let the spirit of Simeon's prayer touch your spirit: "Now at the end of this day, dismiss your servant in peace. Throughout this day I have witnessed your saving deeds." Visualize the saving deeds you have experienced this day, and let them be a silent blessing.

O Light of revelation,

When dawn shows its face and when the shades of twilight enfold me, may I receive the peace that comes from being in communion with you. You who are a window to the eternal, hold me in your view. Don't ever let me out of sight. Death will hold no terror for me, sheltered under your wings. May I rest in peace in life and in death.

Your teacher for this week is *the reality of your death*. How can death be your teacher?

A deathbed is such a special and sacred place:
a deathbed is more like an altar than a bed.
It is an altar where the flesh and blood of a life
is transformed into eternal spirit. . . .
We should endeavor to be present there
with the most contemplative, priestly grace.

–John O'Donohue

CONCLUSION
EVER FLOWING

You have just completed a pilgrimage through the fifty-two weeks of the year. Accompanied by a medley of teachers, you journeyed with the Word of God and found grace as you opened the ear of your heart to listen to your guides. My hope is that you will close the pages of this book with simple joy because of the ever-flowing nature of learning and the abundant ways to absorb the message rather than with the mindset that you are finished. Your next breath is just arriving. Your next insight might become your next teacher. New guides will be following you through your moments, days, weeks, and months.

The flowing grace of now is never finished. It is ever flowing into the next grace, the next joy, the next awakening, the next sorrow, and the next piece of unfolding life. In her novel *The Finishing*

School, Gail Godwin reiterates the truth that it is not death or growing old we ought to fear. Rather, she suggests that what we need to fear is congealing. Congealing is not flowing; it is solidifying. If you are gelatin, that's just fine. However, if you are a living, breathing human being, you will want to be cautious about congealing because it suggests that you have finished growing. There is no more flowing. It is as though the stream of grace dries up and all your *nows* are drowned in boredom, apathy, and indifference. All is static.

For a short time in my life I thought God was like that: fixed, unchanging, and indomitable. Gradually, my theological reflection brought me to new vistas of the Divine, and a loving relationship with the Beloved began to soften the static image of long ago. God became a surprising dance of life, a wind of wonder, a flowing stream, a sweet darkness, and a shimmering light. This is exactly the way I want to be as the pages of my life are turned.

The following prayer has been fashioned into an exquisite melody by songwriter Velma Frye. As you bring these fifty-two weeks of reflection to a close, I encourage you to prayerfully listen to this song, which you can find at www.macrinawieder-kehr.com. The words of this prayer and the song invite you to leap into the flowing grace of God, the flowing grace of life, the flowing grace of now, the flowing grace of all that lives. What better place to be as you come to the end of a year's pilgrimage, only to discover that it's not the end at all? It is ever flowing.

● ● ● ● ● ● ● ● ● ● ● ● ● ● ● ● ● ● ●

O ever-changing God,

Transform me into your flowing grace. Protect me from congealing. Plant deep in my heart an intense desire to be flexible, bendable, and always open to your transforming breath. Ever flowing. Ever flowing. Ever flowing . . . until I flow into the sacred stream of that eternal drink which is you. Then pour me back into the world, and let the flowing begin again and again and again. Ever flowing . . .

● ● ● ● ● ● ● ● ● ● ● ● ● ● ● ● ● ● ●

PERMISSION ACKNOWLEDGMENTS

Early editions of many of the scripture reflections were first printed in *Living Faith: Daily Catholic Devotions*, published quarterly by Creative Communications for the Parish, Inc., 1564 Fencorp Dr., Fenton, MO, 63026, 1-800-325-9414.

SUBJECT INDEX

SCRIPTURE INDEX

Macrina Wiederkehr, O.S.B., is a spiritual guide, popular retreat facilitator, and author who makes her home with the monastic community of St. Scholastica in Fort Smith, Arkansas. The Benedictine traditions of deep listening to the word of God and hospitality toward all of life form the roots of her writing and retreat ministry. Wiederkehr is the bestselling author of nine books, including *Seven Sacred Pauses*, *Abide*, *Behold Your Life*, and *The Circle of Life*, which she coauthored with Joyce Rupp.

macrinawiederkher.com
Facebook: macrina.wiederkehr
Instagram: @MacrinaWiederkehr

AVE

AVE MARIA PRESS

Founded in 1865, Ave Maria Press,
a ministry of the Congregation of
Holy Cross, is a Catholic publishing
company that serves the spiritual and
formative needs of the Church and its
schools, institutions, and ministers;
Christian individuals and families; and
others seeking spiritual nourishment.

For a complete listing of titles from

Ave Maria Press

Sorin Books

Forest of Peace

Christian Classics

visit avemariapress.com